LIFE OF
ABRAHAM LINCOLN

LIFE OF

ABRAHAM LINCOLN

BY W. D. HOWELLS

———◄●►———

*This campaign biography corrected
by the hand of Abraham Lincoln
in the summer of 1860 is reproduced
here with careful attention to
the appearance of the
original volume.*

BLOOMINGTON
INDIANA UNIVERSITY PRESS
1960

CONTENTS

INTRODUCTION

ON May 18, 1860, Abraham Lincoln of Illinois defeated William H. Seward of New York for the presidential nomination at the Republican convention in Chicago, amid scenes of wild excitement; at times the noise of competing demonstrations reached such a pitch that some spectators had to cover their ears.

How much William Dean Howells' biography of Lincoln, published later in the year, contributed to his election is problematical. Like most campaign biographies, it was hastily written, and despite its author's distinction it would no doubt have been forgotten long ago had it not been for the fact that one copy of the book was corrected and annotated by Lincoln himself. Since Lincoln was a conscientious workman, we can assume that everything in Howells' book which he did not correct was of an accuracy acceptable to him. Though a few minor errors escaped his attention, the fact remains that this is one of the few writings on Lincoln which can, in a sense, be regarded as autobiographical.

The book containing Lincoln's penciled notes is

now the property of the Illinois State Historical Library, whose trustees have given their consent to the publication of this facsimile edition. An earlier facsimile, published in 1938 by the Abraham Lincoln Association in a limited edition, has long been out of print.

The original volume was entitled *Lives and Speeches of Abraham Lincoln and Hannibal Hamlin*. Only Howells' biography of Lincoln, with the latter's annotations, is reproduced here. The present volume also contains the Editor's Preface to the 1938 edition, giving the background and history of the book; and an eyewitness account of the Chicago convention originally published in 1860 in a volume by Murat Halstead entitled *Caucuses of 1860*.

A complete bibliography of books, pamphlets, and articles about Lincoln would probably list 15,000 to 20,000 items. We have reached a point in Lincoln scholarship where each new book about the Emancipator needs to be justified. Almost all recent work on Lincoln, even when based on lengthy and tedious research, has, at best, done little more than add minute details to a picture already clearly drawn. Too often recent studies merely rehash information readily available in published works, or are compilations of material better left uncollected. But perhaps the greatest danger is the substitution of antiquarianism for true research and for the maturity of opinion from which fresh interpretations can develop.

In 1936 the late James G. Randall published an admirable essay in the *American Historical Review* entitled "Is the Lincoln Theme Exhausted?" Dr. Randall pointed out how much then remained to be done. One cannot help believing, however, that any essay with the same title today would reach a very different conclusion.

The study of Lincoln is the study of the middle period of American history, a period in our national life when social evolution strode hand in hand with violent revolution. To use Lincoln as the central figure in the middle period is to study problems of the midwestern frontier, the beginnings of urbanization, the coming of the railroads, the dissolution and realignment of political parties, immigration and the westward movement—in short, to study much of the exciting sweep and drama of American history. And, of course, to study Lincoln is to examine a man of grand and noble character, who has served as a model and an inspiration for almost a hundred years.

So the study of Lincoln may properly be the study of one remarkable man, but it ought also to be the study of a critical period in American history: an era of national growing pains whose scope ranges from frontier crudity to White House elegance and from the Missouri Compromise to the Emancipation Proclamation.

But, unfortunately, Lincoln scholarship today can no longer approach the Emancipator in these terms. This ground is already well cultivated. The opening of the Robert Todd Lincoln Papers, and their inclusion in *The Collected Works of Abraham Lincoln,* edited by Roy P. Basler, Marion D. Pratt and Lloyd A. Dunlap (Rutgers University Press, 1953), the masterful one-volume *Abraham Lincoln* by the late Benjamin P. Thomas, and the completion in 1955 of the late Dr. Randall's *Lincoln the President,* filled in the major gaps in the over-all picture. There seems to be no significant unexploited manuscript collection of Lincolniana; very little has been discovered since the *Collected Works* was published. For our generation the work is done.

Even so, we shall continue to study Lincoln. The public appetite for information about our most striking folk hero is perhaps evidence of national maturity. It is also part of the never-ending search for the key to true greatness. Why this country produced a great man at a time when greatness was needed, we really do not know. And we shall keep on trying to plumb the secret of greatness by studying Abraham Lincoln.

CLYDE C. WALTON

Springfield, Illinois

EDITOR'S PREFACE

TO 1938 EDITION

"I WROTE the life of Lincoln which elected him," remarked William Dean Howells to Mark Twain in 1876. Howells had just contracted for a campaign biography of Rutherford B. Hayes and was humorously recalling the past to his friend.

In 1860 Howells, then a young man of twenty-three, was working as an editorial writer on the *Ohio State Journal* at Columbus. Except for a book of poems, *The Lives and Speeches of Abraham Lincoln and Hannibal Hamlin* was the first of the one hundred and three books that Howells wrote during the years from 1860 to 1920. Though he attended neither high school nor university, Howells received degrees from six universities, including Oxford, and rejected offers of professorship in literature from Yale, Harvard and Johns Hopkins universities.

Howells, for many years, was editor of the *Atlantic Monthly* and was a contributing editor of *Harpers.* He was the founder of the school of American realists, presenting with truth and minuteness, the every day aspects of the life and character of the American people. He was the leader of American letters during the quarter century which ended in 1920. In recognition of his writing the campaign biography Lincoln appointed him consul at Venice.

When the book appeared in the summer of 1860, Lincoln, at the request of Samuel C. Parks of Lincoln, Illinois, read the book and made corrections with pencilled notations on the margins.[1] The first ninety-four pages were devoted to the biography of Lincoln and this part of the book is reprinted here in facsimile. The remainder contained some of Mr. Lincoln's speeches and a biographical sketch of Hannibal Hamlin.

Prior to 1860 Lincoln had prepared two autobiographical sketches. The facts, as he gave them, were accurate but limited in scope. The Howells biography, as corrected by Lincoln, is, in effect, a fourth autobiography, and it gives an approved version of several incidents in Lincoln's life before his nomination for the Presidency.

Samuel C. Parks, born in Vermont, moved with his parents to Madison, Indiana, in 1821. Here he attended his father's academy and later, Indiana University, where his father was then a professor of languages. In the spring of 1840, Samuel moved to Springfield, Illinois, and read law in the office of Stuart and Edwards. That fall his father moved to Springfield and opened a private academy, and later became the first superintendent of schools.

Young Parks became a friend of Lincoln and after his own removal to the town of Lincoln, Illinois, he was associated with Lincoln in the trial of many cases in the Logan County Circuit Court. Parks, like Lincoln, became a Republican and

[1] "A Unique Biography of Lincoln," by Benjamin P. Thomas, Abraham Lincoln Association *Bulletin* No. 35.

worked assiduously for the Republican cause. On several occasions, he introduced Lincoln when the latter made speeches in Logan County. He worked for Lincoln's nomination at Chicago; and in 1863, Lincoln appointed him an Associate Justice of the Supreme Court of Idaho Territory. One of the last official acts performed by President Lincoln, on April 14, 1865, was the acceptance of the resignation of Judge Parks. Parks's copy of Howells is now owned by his son, Samuel C. Parks, Jr., of Cody, Wyoming, and he has kindly permitted the Abraham Lincoln Association to reprint it.

When the publishing house of Follett, Foster and Co. employed Howells to write a life of Lincoln, they expected him to go to Springfield to secure material. "This part of the project was distasteful to me," wrote Howells long afterwards. "I would not go, and I missed the greatest chance of my life, of its kind, though I am not sure that I was wholly wrong, for I might not have been equal to the chance; I might not have seemed, to the man I would not go to see, the person to report him to the world in a campaign life. What we did was to commission a young law student I knew, to go to Springfield and get the material for me. When he brought it back, I felt the charm of the material, the wild charm and poetry of its reality was not unknown to me; I was at home with it, for I had known the belated backwoods of a certain region in Ohio; I had almost lived the pioneer; and I wrote the little book with none of the reluctance I felt from studying its sources."

The young law student Howells had sent to Springfield to collect material for the book was James Quay Howard. Born in Ohio in 1840, Howard was not yet of age, though a graduate of Marietta College. He spent some days in Springfield; and Lincoln gave him a copy of the biographical material which he had prepared at the request of John Locke Scripps, of the Chicago *Press and Tribune*. Howard interviewed some of Lincoln's friends in Springfield, George Close, Lincoln's rail-splitting partner in Macon County and his old New Salem friends. He also made some inspection of the files of the *Sangamo Journal* and the *Journal* of the General Assembly of Illinois, before returning to Columbus on June 7, 1860. The extent of his investigations are more clearly revealed in his own campaign biography which Follett, Foster and Co. issued a month after the Howells book. Both authors leaned heavily on the *Debates of Lincoln and Douglas,* which was issued by the same publisher and was in its fourth printing before Lincoln's nomination.

The pre-convention sale of the *Debates* overtaxed the production facilities of the publishers. When Lincoln was nominated, they doubled their capacity, and announced a campaign life of Lincoln (Howells) to be bound in cloth; and also a cheap paper covered edition. At the end of May, the publishers dropped the idea of the edition in paper covers; but before June was half over, their competitors were flooding the market with cheap paper-backed campaign "Lives." They then announced a forthcoming campaign life in paper covers, "entirely distinct" from the Howells book. This was *The Life of Abraham Lincoln* by Howard. Days passed, and it did not appear. The publishers were bogged down with the *Debates* and the Howells book. To appease disgruntled agents, a stop gap measure was adopted. An abbreviated edition of Howells was brought out in paper covers on June 25th. It was a crude affair of 170 pages. Few copies were sold, and today it is a major Lincolniana rarity; but, no doubt it served its purpose, for Howard's book did not appear until July 26th, long after any demand for a new campaign life had ceased to exist.

Though the complete Howells book was not yet published, the publishers were busy stimulating interest and seeking agents for its sale. They announced that Lincoln had authorized the Howells book. This announcement aroused the Ohio Republican leaders; and one of them, Samuel Galloway, queried Lincoln about the authorization. Lincoln replied on June 19th in a letter marked "Especially Confidential," that "Messrs. Follett, Foster & Co's. *Life* of me is *not* by my authority; and I have scarcely been so much astounded by anything as their public announcement that it is authorized by me. . . . I certainly knew they contemplated publishing a biography, and I certainly did not object to their doing so, *upon their own responsibility.* I even took pains to facilitate them. But, at the same time, I made myself tiresome, if not hoarse, with repeating to Mr. Howard . . . that I authorized *nothing,* would be *responsible for nothing* . . . I

would authorize no biography without time and opportunity to carefully examine and consider every
word of it . . . I barely suggest that you, or any
of the friends there, on the party account, look it
over, and exclude what you may think would em-
barrass the party. . . ."[2]

The following editorial in the *Illinois State
Journal,* June 15th, was doubtless inspired by
Lincoln: "We observe that various publishing
houses in different parts of the country are advertis-
ing the 'Life of Mr. Lincoln as nearly ready,' 'in
press,' etc., and prefacing their announcements
with the statement that theirs is the 'authorized'
or the 'only authorized,' 'or the only authentic and
authorized' edition. Now there has been great com-
petition for the publication of Mr. Lincoln's biography, and various parties have been here
procuring the materials for such a work, but it is
unnecessary, we presume, for us to say that none of
them are 'authorized' by Mr. Lincoln. He is ig-
norant of their contents, and is not responsible for
anything they may contain."

The Howells biography was issued on July 5th,
1860.[3] On the 16th of July, the *Illinois State
Journal,* carried the following paragraph : "We are
indebted to the publishers, Messrs. Follett, Foster
and Co., of Columbus, Ohio, for an advanced copy

[2] Lincoln to Samuel Galloway, Springfield, Ill., June 19,
1860. The original letter is in the Illinois State Historical
Library.

[3] Ernest J. Wessen, "Campaign Lives of Abraham Lincoln,"
*Papers in Illinois History and Transactions for the year of
1937.*

of *The Lives of Lincoln and Hamlin,* by Howells and Hayes. It is a neatly printed book of 406 pages, bound in muslin, and altogether got up in good style. The narrative, so far as we have examined, is written in an entertaining manner, and is perhaps as authentic as any biographies of Mr. Lincoln and Mr. Hamlin, which have yet been published. We observe, however, one most egregious and almost unpardonable blunder on page 74. It consists in quoting as the platform of a Republican State Convention purporting to have been held in Springfield in 1854, the very identical *bogus* resolutions which Mr. Douglas attempted to palm off on his public at the first joint discussions at Ottawa, and which he was compelled to take back." This same error had appeared on page 33 of the *Wide Awake Edition,* a campaign biography by an anonymous author, which had recently been issued by Thayer and Eldridge of Boston.

Mr. Lincoln was as much disturbed, no doubt, as the newspaper. He had refuted this claim of Douglas at Ottawa, Freeport and Galesburg. At the latter place, he had gone into detail to forestall Douglas's effort to fix upon him this charge of extreme abolitionism. He carefully pointed out that the resolutions were those of a meeting in Kane County, Illinois, and not of the Republican State Convention held in October, 1854, in Springfield. Lincoln went on to assure the crowd that he had not been associated with either meeting in any way. It is probable that Lincoln carefully read and corrected this volume with the object of having the most glaring errors corrected in later editions. The book was printed from plates and an examination of later editions shows that, with the exception of the footnote on page 33, this was the only error corrected. An errata slip was inserted, facing page 74, in the volumes printed but remaining in the publisher's hands. This eight line correction read as follows: "The resolutions said to have been passed at a convention at Springfield, and found on page 74, were not passed. They were a political trick, invented by the Democrats, to defeat Yates, candidate for Congress. See Douglas and Lincoln Debates, pages 90, 97, 98, 182, 189, 195, 196, 199, 200. This error, in the hurry of going to press, crept in. On page 75, it will be seen, Mr. Lincoln is shown to have had no connection with the resolutions." In one edition, the five lines on page 74, to which Mr. Lincoln objected, were corrected and the page references to the *Debates* placed in a footnote on page 75.

Lincoln read and corrected Parks's copy with characteristic care, many of his corrections are minute. These corrections, made in pencil, can be noted on pages 18, 19, 23, 26, 27, 38, 40, 41, 47, 48, 57, 73, 74 and 93. He made two slight corrections in his speeches, crossing out the word "with" and inserting "in" on page 181, and inserting the word "us" for "it" on page 201.

A few minor mistakes escaped Lincoln's attention. The statement on page 23 that the Lincolns settled "about ten miles northwest of Decatur," should have been "southwest of Decatur." In the footnote on page 24, "James Hawks" should read "James Hanks." Lincoln's modesty did not compel him to comment on two lavish statements on page 31. Here he is set forth as "one of the best informed, as he is certainly the ablest, man in Illinois," and "it is said he has now by heart every line of his favorite poet [Burns]."

The assertion on page 32 that Lincoln was the only person in the New Salem community "equal to the task of making out the mail returns," for the Post Office Department, is obviously untrue, and perhaps that is the reason why Lincoln made no comment on it.

Lincoln did not remain at the head of the Clary Grove Boys throughout the Black Hawk War, as stated on page 35. He announced his candidacy for the Illinois Legislature on March 9, 1832, almost five months before election day, August 6th, although Howells says, on page 40 that he announced it only ten days before the election. Lincoln did not receive the largest vote of any candidate in the 1834 election as Howells indicated on page 41. John Dawson received 1390 votes to 1376 for Lincoln. This error was repeated on page 44.

In a footnote on page 42, Howells gives the middle initial of William G. Greene as "T" after having it correct in a footnote on page 39. Lincoln corrected the middle initial in John T. Stuart's name on page 48, but failed to correct it on the preceding page.

The partnership of Stuart and Lincoln (page 49) did not terminate on Stuart's election to Congress in August, 1838, but continued to the spring of 1841.

Howells suggested on page 78 that the Lincoln-Douglas debates had been so significant in their results that United States Senators in Illinois would thereafter be elected by the people instead of the legislature. Illinois history subsequent to 1860 does not bear out Howells's prophecy.

One statement that Lincoln did not correct is inconsistent with the third person autobiography that Lincoln wrote for John L. Scripps in 1860. Howells said that when Lincoln first began surveying, he used a grapevine instead of a chain; whereas Lincoln stated in the autobiography: ''The surveyor of Sangamon County offered to depute to Abraham that portion of his work which was within his part of the County. He accepted, procured a compass and chain, studied Flint and Gibson a little, and went at it.'' These oversights are so few and of such a minor character that we can conclude that most of the statements that Lincoln did not contradict are true. Thus the book becomes a valuable historical source and enables us to speak with more assurance on several hitherto uncertain points in the pre-presidential period of Lincoln's life. Howells declared, for example, that ''when practicing law, before his election to Congress, a copy of Burns was his inseparable companion on the Circuit. . . . He is also a diligent student of Shakespeare. . . . The bent of his mind, however, is mathematical and metaphysical, and he is . . . therefore pleased with the absolute and logical method of Poe's tales and sketches, in which the problem of mystery is given, and wrought out into everyday facts by the processes of cunning analysis. It is said that he suffers no year to pass without a perusal of this author.'' We can conclude that he was an enthusiastic reader of these three authors. His liking of Poe's detective stories is especially noteworthy. Howells states that Lincoln received fifteen dollars a month for clerking in Offut's store and that the first publication for which he subscribed was the *Louisville Journal.*

Howells described Lincoln's parents as ''poor, even for that rude time and country; and, as a child, Thomas made acquaintance only with hardship and privation. He was a wandering, homeless boy, working when he could find work, and enduring when he could not. He grew up without education; his sole accomplishment in chirography being his own clumsy signature. . . . From both his parents young Lincoln inherited an iron constitution and a decent poverty. From his father came the knack of story telling, which has made him so delightful among acquaintances, and so irresistible in his stump and forensic drolleries.''

Several stories previously based only on traditional evidence, are substantiated by this book. One is the story that Lincoln, while living in Macon County, discomfited two visiting political candidates, W. L. D. Ewing and a man named Posey, with an impromptu reply to their speeches; another is the story of Lincoln walking eight miles, while at New Salem, to borrow a copy of Kirkham's *Grammar* and of his getting a ''fair, practical knowledge'' of it in three weeks. These appear without contradiction. Howells also tells of Lincoln's receiving the news of his nomination for President in the office of the *Illinois State Journal,* and of his departing with the remark, ''There is a little woman down the street who would like to know something about this.''

There are several versions of Lincoln's famous wrestling match with Jack Armstrong at New Salem. Probably the one most widely accepted is to the effect that after the two men had been struggling for some time Armstrong, beginning to get the worst of it, resorted to a foul, that so enraged Lincoln that he lifted Armstrong in the air, shook him as he would a dog, and threw him to the ground; that Armstrong's friends rushed at Lincoln; but that Armstrong, admitting that Lincoln had fairly beaten him, commanded them to stand back. Howells made no mention of a foul, but stated that when Armstrong began to get the worst of it, the Clary Grove Boys rushed in to help him; that Lincoln refused to continue against such odds, but offered to wrestle, race or fight any of them individually, and that finally Lincoln and Armstrong agreed to call the match a draw. Lincoln, in reading Howells, let this stand unchanged. If Armstrong did commit a foul, Lincoln preferred not to claim it, and if he defeated Armstrong he also made no mention of that fact.

In telling of Lincoln's experiences in the Black Hawk War, Howells related the story of the old Indian who wandered into camp and was seized by volunteer soldiers, who threatened to kill him. This Indian had a letter from General Cass certifying that he was friendly to the whites, but that meant nothing to the hard-headed pioneer soldiers, who would have carried out their threat if Lincoln had not intervened. Lincoln demanded that they let the man go; and when they accused him of cowardice, offered to convince any of them to the contrary. This story was based on tradition, and Albert J. Beveridge, among others, regarded it as improbable, but Lincoln read it without contradicting it.

By accepting Howells's statement that while living at New Salem "he bought an old copy of Blackstone, one day, at an auction in Springfield," Lincoln inferentially refuted the story of his having providentially discovered a copy of Blackstone at the bottom of a barrel of junk that he bought from a passing traveler to help him on his way.

Lincoln borrowed the Howells book from the Library of Congress on May 4, 1864, returning it on May 31, and took it out again on March 22, 1865. The book was at the White House at the time of Lincoln's assassination, as it was not returned until May 3, 1865.

Twenty years after writing the campaign biography, Howells penned this tribute to Lincoln:

> "No admirer who speaks in his praise must pause to conceal a stain upon his good name. No true man falters in his affection at the remembrance of any mean action or littleness in the life of Lincoln. The purity of his reputation ennobles every incident of his career and gives significance to all events of his past."

ABRAHAM LINCOLN ASSOCIATION.

LINCOLN IS NOMINATED:

AN EYEWITNESS ACCOUNT

———————◆•●•◆———————

From Murat Halstead, *Caucuses of 1860: A History of the National Political Conventions of the Current Presidential Campaign* (Columbus, Ohio, 1860), pp. 141-49.

THIRD day [May 18, 1860].—After adjournment on Thursday (the second day) there were few men in Chicago who believed it possible to prevent the nomination of Seward. His friends had played their game to admiration and had been victorious on every preliminary skirmish. When the platform had been adopted, inclusive of the Declaration of Independence, they felt themselves already exalted upon the pinnacle of victory. They rejoiced exceedingly, and full of confidence, cried in triumphant tones, "Call the roll of States." But it was otherwise ordered. . . . The opponents of Mr. Seward left the wigwam that evening thoroughly disheartened. Greeley was, as has been widely reported, absolutely "terrified." The nomination of Seward in defiance of his influence would have been a cruel blow. He gave up the ship. . . .

The New Yorkers were exultant. Their bands were playing and the champagne flowing at their headquarters as after a victory.

But there was much done after midnight and before the convention assembled on Friday morning. There were hundreds of Pennsylvanians, Indianians and Illinoisans, who never closed their eyes that night. I saw Henry S. Lane at one o'clock, pale and haggard, with cane under his arm, walking as if for a wager, from one caucus room to another, at the Tremont House. He had been toiling with desperation to bring the Indiana delegation to go as a unit for Lincoln. And then in connection with others, he had been operating to bring the Vermonters and Virginians to the point of deserting Seward. . . .

The Seward men generally abounded in confidence Friday morning. The air was full of rumors of the caucusing the night before, but the opposition of the doubtful states to Seward was an old story; and after the distress of Pennsylvania, Indiana & Co., on the subject of Seward's availability, had been so freely and ineffectually expressed from the start, it was not imagined their protests would suddenly become effective. The Sewardites marched as usual from their headquarters at the Richmond House after their magnificent band, which was brilliantly uniformed—epaulets shining on their shoulders and white and scarlet feathers waving from their caps—marched under the orders of recognized leaders, in a style that would have done credit to many volunteer military companies. They were about a thousand strong, and protracting their march a little too far, were not all able to get into the wigwam. This was their first misfortune. They were not where they could scream with the best effect in responding to the mention of the name of William H. Seward.

When the Convention was called to order, breathless attention was given the proceedings. There was not a space a foot square in the wigwam unoccupied. There were tens of thousands still outside, and torrents of men had rushed in at the three broad doors until not another one could squeeze in. . . .

Everybody was now impatient to begin the work. Mr. Evarts of New York nominated Mr. Seward. Mr. Judd of Illinois nominated Mr. Lincoln. . . .

Everybody felt that the fight was between them and yelled accordingly.

The applause when Mr. Evarts named Seward was enthusiastic. When Mr. Judd named Lincoln, the response was prodigious, rising and raging far beyond the Seward shriek. Presently, upon Caleb B. Smith seconding the nomination of Lincoln, the response was absolutely terrific. It now became the Seward men to make another effort, and when Blair of Michigan seconded his nomination,

> At once there rose so wild a yell,
> Within that dark and narrow dell;
> As all the fiends from heaven that fell
> Had pealed the banner cry of hell.

The effect was startling. Hundreds of persons stopped their ears in pain. The shouting was absolutely frantic, shrill and wild. No Comanches, no panthers, ever struck a higher note or gave screams with more infernal intensity. Looking from the stage over the vast amphitheatre, nothing was to be seen below but thousands of hats—a black, mighty swarm of hats—flying with the velocity of hornets over a mass of human heads, most of the mouths of which were open. Above, all around the galleries, hats and handkerchiefs were flying in the tempest together. The wonder of the thing was that the Seward outside pressure should, so far from New York, be so powerful.

Now the Lincoln men had to try it again, and as Mr. Delano of Ohio on behalf "of a portion of the delegation of that State" seconded the nomination of Lincoln, the uproar was beyond description. Imagine all the hogs ever slaughtered in Cincinnati giving their death squeals together, a score of big steam whistles going (steam at 160 lbs. per inch), and you conceive something of the same nature. I thought the Seward yell could not be surpassed, but the Lincoln boys were clearly ahead and, feeling their victory, as there was a lull in the storm, took deep breaths all round and gave a concentrated shriek that was positively awful, and accompanied it with stamping that made every plank and pillar in the building quiver.

Henry S. Lane of Indiana leaped upon a table, and swinging hat and cane, performed like an acrobat. The presumption is he shrieked with the rest, as his mouth was desperately wide open; but no one will ever be able to testify that he has positive knowledge of the fact that he made a particle of noise. His individual voice was lost in the aggregate hurricane.

The New York, Michigan and Wisconsin delegations sat together and were in the tempest very quiet. Many of their faces whitened as the Lincoln *yawp* swelled into a wild hosanna of victory.

The convention now proceeded to business. . . . The most significant vote was that of Virginia, which had been expected solid for Seward and which now gave him but eight and gave Lincoln fourteen. The New Yorkers looked significantly at each other as this was announced. Then Indiana gave her twenty-six votes for Lincoln. This solid vote was a startler. . . . The division of the first vote caused a fall in Seward stock. It was seen that Lincoln, Cameron and Bates had the strength to defeat Seward, and it was known that the greater part of the Chase vote would go for Lincoln.

The convention proceeded to a second ballot. Every man was fiercely enlisted in the struggle. The partisans of the various candidates were strung up to such a pitch of excitement as to render them incapable of patience, and the cries of "Call the roll" were fairly hissed through their teeth. The first gain for Lincoln was in New Hampshire. The Chase and the Frémont vote from that State were given him. His next gain was the whole vote of Vermont. This was a blighting blow upon the Seward interest. The New Yorkers started as if an Orsini bomb had exploded. And presently the Cameron vote of Pennsylvania was thrown for Lincoln, increasing his strength forty-four votes. The fate of the day was now determined. New York saw "checkmate" next move, and sullenly proceeded with the game, assuming unconsciousness of her inevitable doom. On this ballot Lincoln gained seventy-nine votes! Seward had 184½ votes, Lincoln 181. . . .

While this [the third] ballot was taken amid excitement that tested the nerves, the fatal defection from Seward in New England still further appeared—four votes going over from Seward to Lincoln in Massachusetts. The latter received four additional votes from Pennsylvania and fifteen additional votes from Ohio. It was whispered about: "Lincoln's the coming man—will be nominated this ballot." When the roll of States and Territories had been called, I had ceased to give attention to any votes but those for Lincoln, and had his vote added up as it was given. The number of votes necessary to a choice were two hundred and thirty-three, and I saw under my pencil as the Lincoln column was completed the figures 231½— one vote and a half to give him the nomination. In a moment the fact was whispered about. A hundred pencils had told the same story. The news went over the house wonderfully, and there was a pause. There are always men anxious to distinguish themselves on such occasions. There is nothing that politicians like better than a crisis. I looked up to see who would be the man to give the decisive vote. . . . In about ten ticks of a watch, Cartter of Ohio was up. I had imagined Ohio would be slippery enough for the crisis. And sure enough! Every eye was on Cartter, and everybody who understood the matter at all knew what he was about to do. . . . He said: "I rise (eh), Mr. Chairman (eh), to announce the change of four votes of Ohio from Mr. Chase to Mr. Lincoln." The deed was done. There was a moment's silence. The nerves of the thousands, which through the hours of suspense had been subjected to terrible tension, relaxed, and as deep breaths of relief were taken, there was a noise in the wigwam like the rush of a great wind in the van of a storm— and in another breath, the storm was there. There were thousands cheering with the energy of insanity.

A man who had been on the roof and was engaged in communicating the results of the ballotings to the mighty mass of outsiders now demanded, by gestures at the skylight over the stage, to know what had happened. One of the Secretaries, with a tally sheet in his hands, shouted: "Fire the Salute! Abe Lincoln is nominated!"

The city was wild with delight. The "Old Abe" men formed processions and bore rails through the streets. Torrents of liquor were poured down the throats of the multitude. A hundred guns were fired from the top of the Tremont House. . . .

I left the city on the night train on the Fort Wayne and Chicago road. The train consisted of eleven cars, every seat full and people standing in the aisles and corners. I never before saw a company of persons so prostrated by continued excitement. The Lincoln men were not able to respond to the cheers which went up along the road for "Old Abe." They had not only done their duty in that respect, but exhausted their capacity. At every station where there was a village, until after two o'clock, there were tar barrels burning, drums beating, boys carrying rails, and guns, great and small, banging away. The weary passengers were allowed no rest, but plagued by the thundering jar of cannon, the clamor of drums, the glare of bonfires, and the whooping of the boys, who were delighted with the idea of a candidate for the Presidency who thirty years ago split rails on the Sangamon River —classic stream now and forevermore—and whose neighbors named him "honest."

This life of Lincoln was
corrected by him for me, at my
request, in the summer of 1860,
by notes in his hand writing in
pencil, on the margin.

It is to be preserved by my
children, as a lasting memorial
of that great man, and of his
friendship for me.

Samuel C. Parks.

Kansas City, Mo.
May 22nd, 1901.

Photograph by M.B. Brady

Eng.d by J.C.Buttre, N.Y.

A. Lincoln

LIVES AND SPEECHES

OF

ABRAHAM LINCOLN

AND

HANNIBAL HAMLIN.

———•———

COLUMBUS, O.:

FOLLETT, FOSTER & CO.

BOSTON: CROSBY, NICHOLS, LEE & CO.

1860.

LIFE

OF

ABRAHAM LINCOLN.

BY

W. D. HOWELLS.

2

PREFACE.

WHEN one has written a hurried book, one likes to dwell upon the fact, that if the time had not been wanting one could have made it a great deal better.

This fact is of the greatest comfort to the author, and not of the slightest consequence to anybody else.

It is perfectly reasonable, therefore, that every writer should urge it.

A work which seeks only to acquaint people with the personal history of a man for whom they are asked to cast their votes—and whose past ceases to concern them in proportion as his present employs them—will not be numbered with those immortal books which survive the year of their publication. It does not challenge criticism; it fulfills the end of its being if it presents facts and incidents in a manner not altogether barren of interest.

It is believed that the following biographical sketch of ABRAHAM LINCOLN will be found reliable. The information upon which the narrative is based, has been derived chiefly from the remembrance of MR. LINCOLN'S old friends, and may, therefore, be considered authentic. It is hardly necessary to add, that no one but the writer is responsible for his manner of treating events and men.

LIFE OF ABRAHAM LINCOLN.

———————·———————

CHAPTER I.

IT is necessary that every American should have an indisputable grandfather, in order to be represented in the Revolutionary period by actual ancestral service, or connected with it by ancestral reminiscence. Further back than a grandfather few can go with satisfaction. Everything lies wrapt in colonial obscurity and confusion; and you have either to claim that the Smiths came over in the Mayflower, or that the Joneses were originally a Huguenot family of vast wealth and the gentlest blood; or that the Browns are descended from the race of Powhattan in the direct line; or you are left in an extremely embarrassing uncertainty as to the fact of great-grandparents.

We do not find it profitable to travel far into the past in search of Abraham Lincoln's ancestry. There is a dim possibility that he is of the stock of the New England Lincolns, of Plymouth colony; but the noble science of heraldry is almost obsolete in this country, and

(17)

none of Mr. Lincoln's family seems to have been aware of the preciousness of long pedigrees, so that the records are meagre.   The first that is known of his forefathers is that they were Quakers, who may have assisted in those shrewd bargains which honest William Penn drove with the Indians, for we find them settled at an early day in the old county of Berks, in Pennsylvania, where doubtless some of their descendants yet remain. Whether these have fallen away from the calm faith of their ancestors is not a matter of history, but it is certain that the family from which the present Abraham Lincoln derives his lineage, long ago ceased to be Quaker in everything but its devout Scriptural names.   His grandfather, (anterior to whom is incertitude, and absolute darkness of names and dates,) was born in Rockingham county, Virginia, whither part of the family had emigrated from Pennsylvania; and had four brothers, patriarchially and apostolically named Isaac, Jacob, John, and Thomas; himself heading the list as Abraham Lincoln.

The descendants of Jacob and John, if any survive, still reside in Virginia; Thomas settled in the Cumberland region, near the adjunction of North Carolina, Tennessee, and Virginia, and very probably his children's children may there be found.   Late in the last century, Abraham, with his wife and five children, removed from Rockingham to Kentucky, at a time when the border was the scene of savage warfare between the Indians and the whites, and when frontier life was

diversified by continual incursions, repulsions, and re-
prisals, on one side and on the other. In one of these
frequent invasions, Abraham Lincoln was killed by
the Indians, who stole upon him while he was at work
and shot him. There is historical mention made of an
Indian expedition to Hardin county, Kentucky, in 1781,
which resulted in the massacre of some of the settlers;
but the date of Lincoln's death is fixed some three years
later, and there is no other account of it than family
tradition.

His wife, his three sons and two daughters survived
him; but the dispersion of his family soon took place;
the daughters marrying, and the sons seeking their fortunes in different localities. Of the latter, Thomas Lincoln, the father of Abraham Lincoln of to-day, was the
youngest, and doubtless felt more severely than the rest
the loss which had befallen them. They were poor,
even for that rude time and country; and as a child,
Thomas made acquaintance only with hardship and privation. He was a wandering, homeless boy, working
when he could find work, and enduring when he could
not. He grew up without education; his sole accomplishment in chirography being his own clumsy signature. At twenty-eight he married Lucy Hanks, and *Nancy*
settled in Hardin county, where, on the 12th of Feb-
ruary, 1809, ABRAHAM LINCOLN was born.

Lincoln's mother was, like his father, Virginian; but
beyond this, little or nothing is known of her. From
both his parents young Lincoln inherited an iron con-

stitution and a decent poverty. From his father came that knack of story-telling, which has made him so delightful among acquaintances, and so irresistible in his stump and forensic drolleries. It is a matter of some regret that the information with regard to Thomas Lincoln and his wife is so meager. The information is, however, not altogether necessary to the present history, and the conjecture to which one is tempted would be as idle as impertinent. It is certain that Lincoln cherished, with just pride, a family repute for native ability, and alluded to it in after life, when he felt the first impulses of ambition, and began in earnest his struggle with the accidents of ignorance and poverty.

A younger brother of Abraham's died in infancy; and a sister, older than himself, married and died many years ago. With her he attended school during his early childhood in Kentucky, and acquired the alphabet, and other rudiments of education. The schooling which Abraham then received from the books and birch of Zachariah Riney and Caleb Hazel, (of pedagogic memory,) and afterward from Azel W. Dorsey,* and one or two others in Indiana, amounted in time to nearly a year, and can not be otherwise computed. It is certain, however, that this brief period limits his scholastic course. Outside of it, his education took place through the rough and wholesome experiences of border

---

*This gentleman is still living in Schuyler county, Illinois.

life, the promptings of a restless ambition, and a profound love of knowledge for its own sake. Under these influences, he has ripened into a hardy physical manhood, and acquired a wide and thorough intelligence, without the aid of schools or preceptors.

In the autumn of 1816, when Abraham was eight years old, his father determined to quit Kentucky. Already the evil influences of slavery were beginning to be felt by the poor and the non-slaveholders. But the emigration of Thomas Lincoln is, we believe, to be chiefly attributed to the insecurity of the right by which he held his Kentucky land; for, in those days, land-titles were rather more uncertain than other human affairs. Abandoning his old home, and striking through the forests in a northwesterly direction, he fixed his new dwelling-place in the heart of the " forest primeval " of what is now Spencer county, Indiana. The dumb solitude there had never echoed to the ax, and the whole land was a wilderness.

The rude cabin of the settler was hastily erected, and then those struggles and hardships commenced which are the common trials of frontier life, and of which the story has been so often repeated. Abraham was a hardy boy, large for his years, and with his ax did manful service in clearing the land. Indeed, with that implement, he literally hewed out his path to manhood; for, until he was twenty-three, the ax was seldom out of his hand, except in the intervals of labor, or when it was exchanged for the plow, the hoe, or the sickle. His youth-

ful experiences in this forest life did not differ from those
familiar to many others.   As an adventurous boy, no
doubt the wood was full of delight and excitement to him.
No doubt he hunted the coon, trapped the turkey, and
robbed the nest of the pheasant.   As a hunter with the
rifle, however, he did not acquire great skill, for he has
never excelled an exploit of his eighth year, when he
shot the leader of a flock of turkeys which ventured
within sight of the cabin during his father's absence.

The family had hardly been two years in their new
home when it was desolated by the death of Abraham's
mother.   This heavy loss was afterward partially re-
paired by the marriage of his father to Mrs. Sally John-
ston, of Elizabethtown, Kentucky.   She was the parent
of three children by a former husband, and was always a
good and affectionate mother to Thomas Lincoln's moth-
erless son.*

The Lincolns continued to live in Spencer county,
until 1830, nothing interrupting the even tenor of Abraham's life, except in his nineteeth year, a flat-boat trip
to New Orleans.   He and a son of the owner composed
the crew, and without other assistance, voyaged

" Down the beautiful river,
Past the Ohio shore, and past the mouth of the Wabash,
Into the golden stream of the broad and swift Mississippi,"

Trafficking here and there, in their course, with the

---

* Mrs. Lincoln is still living, in Coles county, Illinois.

inhabitants, and catching glimpses of the great world so long shut out by the woods. One night, having tied up their "cumbrous boat," near a solitary plantation on the sugar coast, they were attacked and boarded by seven stalwart negroes; but Lincoln and his comrade, after a severe contest in which both were hurt, succeeded in beating their assailants and driving them from the boat. After which they weighed what anchor they had, as speedily as possible, and gave themselves to the middle current again. With this sole adventure, Lincoln resumed his quiet backwoods life in Indiana.

Four years afterward, on the first of March, 1830, his father determined to emigrate once more, and the family abandoned the cabin which had been their home so long, and set out for Illinois. The emigrant company was made up of Thomas Lincoln's family, and the families of Mrs. Lincoln's two sons-in-law. Their means of progress and conveyance were ox-wagons, one of which Abraham Lincoln drove. Before the month was elapsed they had arrived at Macon county, Illinois, where they remained a short time, and Lincoln's family "located" on some new land, about ten miles northwest of Decatur, on the north bank of the Sangamon river, at a junction of forest and prairie land. Here the father and son built a log-cabin, and split rails enough to fence in their land. It is supposed that these are the rails which have since become historic ; though they were by no means the only ones which the robust young backwoodsman made. Indeed, there are other particular rails* which dispute a celebrity somewhat indifferent to the sincere admirer of Mr. Lincoln. The work done was in the course of farm labor, and went to the development of Mr. Lincoln's muscle. Otherwise it is difficult to perceive how it has affected his career.

---

* Mr. George Close, the partner of Lincoln in the rail-splitting business, says that Lincoln was, at this time, a farm laborer, working from day to day, for different people, chopping wood, mauling rails, or doing whatever was to be done. The country was poor, and hard work was the common lot; the heaviest share falling to young unmarried men, with whom it was a continual struggle to earn a livelihood. Lincoln and Mr. Close made about one thousand rails together, for James Hawks and William Miller, receiving their pay in homespun clothing. Lincoln's bargain with Miller's wife, was, that he should have one yard of brown jeans, (richly dyed with walnut bark,) for every four hundred rails made, until he should have enough for a pair of trowsers. As Lincoln was already of great altitude, the number of rails that went to the acquirement of his pantaloons was necessarily immense.

CHAPTER II.

In his time, Denton Offutt was a man of substance; an enterprising and adventurous merchant, trading between the up-river settlements and the city of New Orleans, and fitting out frequent flat-boat expeditions to that cosmopolitan port, where the French voyageur and the rude hunter that trapped the beaver on the Osage and Missouri, met the polished old-world exile, and the tongues of France, Spain, and England made babel in the streets. In view of his experience, it is not too extravagant to picture Denton Offutt as a backwoods Ulysses, wise beyond the home-keeping pioneers about him—

"Forever roaming with a hungry heart,"

bargaining with the Indians, and spoiling them, doubtless, as was the universal custom in those times; learning the life of the wild Mississippi towns, with their lawless frolics, deep potations, and reckless gambling; meeting under his own roof-tree the many-negroed planter of the sugar-coast, and the patriarchal creole of Louisiana; ruling the boatman who managed his craft, and defying the steamboat captain that swept by the slow broad-horn with his stately palace of paint and gilding; with his body inured to toil and privation, and with all

3   (25)

his wits sharpened by traffic; such, no doubt, was Denton
Offutt, who had seen

——" Cities of men,
And manners, climates, councils, governments,"

and such was one of Lincoln's earliest friends. He quick-
ly discovered the sterling qualities of honesty and fidelity,
and the higher qualities of intellect which lay hid under
the young Kentuckian's awkward exterior, and he at
once took Lincoln into his employment. He was now
about sending another flat-boat to New Orleans, and he
engaged Lincoln, and the husband of one of Lincoln's
step-sisters, together with their comrade, John Hanks,*
to take charge of his craft for the voyage from Beardstown, in Illinois, to the Crescent City.

In this winter of 1830–31, a deep snow, long remembered in Illinois, covered the whole land for many weeks,
and did not disappear until the first of March, when the
waters of the thaw inundated the country. Overland
travel from Macon county to Beardstown was rendered
impossible; Lincoln, and his relative, therefore, took a
canoe and descended the Sangamon river to Springfield,
where they found Offutt. He had not succeeded in
getting a flat-boat at Beardstown, as he expected; but
with innumerable flat-boats growing up in their primal
element of timber about him, he was not the man to be
baffled by the trifling consideration that he had no flat-
boat built. He offered to Lincoln and each of his

* Now a well known railroad man in Illinois.

friends, twelve dollars a month for the time they should be occupied in getting out lumber, and making the boat. The offer was accepted. The ax did its work; the planks were sawed ~~with a whip-saw~~; Denton's ark was put together, and the trip to New Orleans triumphantly and profitably made.

On his return to Illinois, Lincoln found that his father had (in pursuance of a previous intention) removed from Macon, and was now living in Coles county. His relative rejoined his family there; but New Salem, on the Sangamon river, became the home of Lincoln, whose "location" there was accidental rather than otherwise. He was descending the river with ~~another~~ flat-boat for Offutt, and near New Salem grounded on a dam. An old friend and ardent admirer, who made his acquaintance on this occasion, says that Lincoln was standing in the water on the dam, when he first caught sight of him, devoting all his energies to the release of the boat. His dress at this time consisted of a pair of blue jeans trowsers indefinitely rolled up, a cotton shirt, striped white and blue, (of the sort known in song and tradition as *hickory*,) and a buckeye-chip hat for which a demand of twelve and a half cents would have been exorbitant.

The future president failed to dislodge his boat; though he did adopt the ingenious expedient of lightening it by boring a hole in the end that hung over the dam and letting out the water—an incident which Mr. Douglas humorously turned to account in one of his speeches. The boat stuck there stubborn, immovable.

Offutt, as has been seen, was a man of resource and decision. He came ashore from his flat-boat and resolutely rented the very mill of which the dam had caused his disaster, together with an old store-room, which he filled with a stock of goods, and gave in the clerkly charge of Abraham Lincoln, with the munificent salary of fifteen dollars a month.

Lincoln had already made his first speech. General W. L. D. Ewing, and a politician named Posey, who afterward achieved notoriety in the Black Hawk war, had addressed the freemen of Macon the year previous, " on the issues of the day." Mr. Posey had, however, in violation of venerable precedent and sacred etiquette, failed to invite the sovereigns to drink something. They were justly indignant, and persuaded Lincoln to reply, in the expectation that he would possibly make himself offensive to Posey. Lincoln, however, took the stump with characteristic modesty, and begging his friends not to laugh if he broke down, treated very courteously the two speakers who had preceded him, discussed questions of politics, and in his peroration eloquently pictured the future of Illinois. There was sense and reason in his arguments, and his imaginative flight tickled the State pride of the Illinoians. It was declared that Lincoln had made the best speech of the day; and he, to his great astonishment, found himself a prophet among those of his own household, while his titled fellow-orator cordially complimented his performance.

At New Salem, he now found the leisure and the

opportunity to initiate a system of self-education. At last, he had struggled to a point, where he could not only take breath, but could stoop and drink from those springs of knowledge, which a hopeless poverty, incessant toil, and his roving, uncertain life, had, till then, forbidden to his lips.

There seems never to have been any doubt of his ability among Lincoln's acquaintances, any more than there was a doubt of his honesty, his generosity, and gentle-heartedness. When, therefore, he began to make rapid progress in his intellectual pursuits, it surprised none of them—least of all, Lincoln's shrewd patron, Offutt, who had been known to declare, with pardonable enthusiasm, that Lincoln was the smartest man in the United States.

The first branch of learning which he took up, was English grammar, acquiring that science from the dry and meager treatise of Kirkham. The book was not to be had in the immediate vicinity, and Lincoln walked seven or eight miles to borrow a copy. He then devoted himself to the study with the whole strength of his resolute nature ; and in three weeks he had gained a fair practical knowledge of the grammar. No doubt the thing was hard to the uncultivated mind, though that mind *was* of great depth and fertility. One of his friends* relates that Lincoln used to take him aside, and require explanations of the sententious Kirkham, whenever he visited New Salem.

---

* L. M. Green, Esq., of Petersburgh, Illinois.

This young backwoodsman had the stubborn notion that because the Lincolns had always been people of excellent sense, he, a Lincoln, might become a person of distinction. He had talked, he said, with men who were regarded as great, and he did not see where they differed so much from others. He reasoned, probably, that the secret of their success lay in the fact of original capacity, and untiring industry. He was conscious of his own powers; he was a logician, and could not resist logical conclusions. If he studied, why might not he achieve?

And Kirkham fell before him. One incident of his study, was a dispute with the learned man of the place, —a very *savant* among the unlettered pioneers—in regard to a grammatical nicety, and the question being referred to competent authority, it was decided in Lincoln's favor, to his pride and exultation.

Concluding his grammatical studies with Kirkham, he next turned his attention to mathematics, and took up a work on surveying, with which he made himself thoroughly acquainted.

So great was his ardor in study, at this time, that shrewd suspicions with regard to Offutt's clerk got abroad; the honest neighbors began to question whether one who would voluntarily spend all his leisure in

———"poring over miserable books,"

could be altogether right in his mind.

The peculiar manner in which he afterward pursued

his law studies, was not calculated to allay popular feeling. He bought an old copy of Blackstone, one day, at auction, in Springfield, and on his return to New Salem, attacked the work with characteristic energy.

His favorite place of study was a wooded knoll near New Salem, where he threw himself under a wide-spreading oak, and expansively made a reading desk of the hillside. Here he would pore over Blackstone day after day, shifting his position as the sun rose and sank, so as to keep in the shade, and utterly unconscious of everything but the principles of common law. People went by, and he took no account of them; the salutations of acquaintances were returned with silence, or a vacant stare; and altogether the manner of the absorbed student was not unlike that of one distraught.

Since that day, his habits of study have changed somewhat, but his ardor remains unabated, and he is now regarded as one of the best informed, as he is certainly the ablest, man in Illinois.

When practicing law, before his election to Congress, a copy of Burns was his inseparable companion on the circuit; and this he perused so constantly, that it is said he has now by heart every line of his favorite poet. He is also a diligent student of Shakspeare, "to know whom is a liberal education."

The bent of his mind, however, is mathematical and metaphysical, and he is therefore pleased with the absolute and logical method of Poe's tales and sketches, in which the problem of mystery is given, and wrought out into every-day facts by processes of cunning analysis. It is said that he suffers no year to pass without the perusal of this author.

Books, of all sorts, the eager student devoured with an insatiable appetite; and newspapers were no less precious to him. The first publication for which he ever sub-scribed, was the *Louisville Journal*, which he paid for when he could secure the intellectual luxury only at the expense of physical comfort.

It was a day of great rejoicing with Lincoln, when President Jackson appointed him postmaster at New Salem. He was a Whig, but the office was of so little pecuniary significance, that it was bestowed irrespective of politics. Lincoln, indeed, was the only person in the community whose accomplishments were equal to the task of making out the mail returns for the Depart-ment.

An acquaintance says that the Presidency can never make our candidate happier than the post-office did then. He foresaw unlimited opportunities for reading newspapers, and of satisfying his appetite for knowl-edge.

But it was not through reading alone that Lincoln cultivated his intellect. The grave and practical Ameri-can mind has always found entertainment and profit in disputation, and the debating clubs are what every American youth is subject to. They are useful in many ways. They safely vent the mental exuberance of youth ; those whom destiny intended for the bar and the Senate, they assist; those who have a mistaken vocation to oratory, they mercifully extinguish.

Even in that day, and that rude country, where learning was a marvelous and fearful exception, the debating school flourished, in part as a literary institution, and in part as a rustic frolic.

Lincoln delighted in practicing polemics, as it was called, and used to walk six and seven miles through the woods to attend the disputations in his neighborhood. Of course, many of the debates were infinitely funny, for the disputants were, frequently, men without education. Here, no doubt, Lincoln stored his mind with anecdote and comic illustration, while he delighted his auditors with his own wit and reason, and added to his growing popularity.

This popularity had been early founded by a stroke of firmness and bravery on Lincoln's part, when he first came into Sangamon county.

He had returned from that famous voyage made with Offutt's impromptu flat-boat to New Orleans, and descending the Sangamon river, had, as has been already related, fixed upon the little village of New Salem,* by fortuity rather than intention, as his future home. Nevertheless, he had first to undergo an ordeal to which every new comer was subjected, before his residence could be generally acknowledged. Then, when it was much more necessary to be equal parts of horse and

---

* Now Petersburgh.

alligator, and to be able to vanquish one's weight in wild cats, than now, there flourished, in the region of New Salem, a band of jolly, roystering blades, calling themselves " Clary's Grove Boys," who not only gave the law to the neighborhood, as Regulators, but united judicial to legislative functions, by establishing themselves a tribunal to try the stuff of every one who came into that region. They were, at once, the protectors and the scourge of the whole country-side, and must have been some such company as that of Brom Bones, in Sleepy Hollow, upon whom the " neighbors all looked with a mixture of awe, admiration, and good-will." Their mode of receiving a stranger was to appoint some one of their number to wrestle with him, fight with him, or run a foot-race with him, according to their pleasure, and his appearance.

As soon as young Lincoln appeared, the " Clary's Grove Boys" determined to signalize their prowess anew by a triumph over a stalwart fellow, who stood six feet three inches without stockings. The leader and champion of their band, (one Jack Armstrong, who seems himself to have been another Brom Bones,) challenged Lincoln to a wrestling-match. When the encounter took place, the " Clary's Grove Boy " found that he had decidedly the worst half of the affair, and the bout would have ended in his ignominious defeat, had not all his fellow-boys come to his assistance. Lincoln then refused to continue the unequal struggle. He would wrestle with them fairly, or he would run a foot-race, or if any of them desired to fight, he generously offered to thrash that particular individual. He looked every word he said, and none of the Boys saw fit to accept his offer. Jack Armstrong was willing to call the match drawn; and Lincoln's fearless conduct had already won the hearts of his enemies. He was invited to become one of their company. His popularity was assured. The Boys idolized him, and when the Black Hawk war broke out, he was chosen their captain, and remained at their head throughout the campaign. Their favor still pursued him, and, at the close of the war, he was elected to the Legislature, through the influence created by his famous wrestling-match.

Many of the Boys are now distinguished citizens of Illinois, and are among Lincoln's warmest friends; though they acknowledge that if he had shown signs of cowardice when they came to the rescue of their champion, it would have fared grievously with him.

Indeed, this seems to have been one of the most significant incidents of his early life. It gave him reputation for courage necessary in a new country, and opened a career to him which his great qualities have enabled him to pursue with brilliance and success.*

---

* Jack Armstrong, in particular, became a fast friend of Lincoln. It is related that he bestowed a terrible pummeling on a person who once ventured to speak slightingly of Lincoln in his presence. Afterward, Lincoln had an opportunity to make a full return to Armstrong for his friendship. A man had been killed in a riot at camp-meeting, in Menard county, and suspicion fell upon a son of Jack Armstrong—a wild young scapegrace, who was known to have taken part in the affair. He was arrested, and brought to trial for murder. Lincoln, who seems to have believed firmly in the young man's innocence, volun-

CHAPTER III.

In 1832, Black Hawk's war broke out. In the light of history, this war seems to have been a struggle involuntarily commenced by the Indians against the white settlers. A treaty had been made by the Sacs and Foxes, ceding to the United States all the land east of the Mississippi—a treaty which the Sac chief, Black Hawk, declared to be illegal. A war with the Sacs ensued, which was terminated by treaty in 1825. Meanwhile Illinois had been admitted to the Union, and the country had filled up with whites, who extended the lines of their settlements around the country of the Indians, and pressed closer and closer upon them. Outrages, on one part and on the other, were of constant occurrence; and in revenge for some wrong, a party of Chippeway Indians fired upon a keel-boat conveying stores to Fort Snelling. Through mistake or injustice, Black Hawk was arrested for this, and lay imprisoned a whole year before he could be brought to trial and acquitted. After his release, it

teered in his defense, and throwing aside the well-connected links of circumstantial evidence against him, made a most touching and eloquent appeal to the sympathies of the jury. There was that confidence in Lincoln, that absolute faith, that he would never say anything but the truth, to achieve any end, that the jury listened and were convinced. Young Armstrong was acquitted; and Lincoln refused to accept any reward for his defense.

was believed that he engaged in negotiations to unite all the Indians, from Rock River to the Gulf of Mexico, in a general war upon the whites. The alarm, of course, was very great, and active preparations for hostilities were made. Regular forces were marched against the Indians at Rock Island, and large bodies of militia were called into the field. It appears that Black Hawk never succeeded in rallying about him more than two or three hundred warriors of his tribe; the Indians being desirous of peace, and willing to abide by the treaty of the chief Keokuk, who favored the cession of land. Indeed, Black Hawk himself attempted to treat with the whites several times when he met them, and only fought after his flags of truce had been fired upon. The war was brought to a close by the battle of Bad-Ax, in which glorious action a great number of squaws and papooses, not to mention several warriors, were killed. The Indians then retreated beyond the Mississippi, and Black Hawk was brought a prisoner into the camp of the whites. He made the grand tour of the Atlantic cities, where he received the usual attentions bestowed upon lions of every tribe, and returning to the West a sadder and a wiser Indian, passed into oblivion.

There can not be any doubt that the war was a very serious matter to the people who were engaged in it; and there is as little doubt that their panic exaggerated their danger, and rendered them merciless in their determination to expel the Indians.

Offutt's business had long been failing, and at the

time the war broke out, Lincoln had the leisure, as well
as the patriotism, to join one of the volunteer companies
which was formed in the neighborhood of New Salem.
To his unbounded surprise and satisfaction, he was
chosen captain by his fellow-soldiers. The place of
rendezvous was at Richland, and as soon as the members of the company met, the election took place. It
was expected that the captaincy would be conferred on
a man of much wealth and consequence among the
people, for whom Lincoln had once worked. He was
a harsh and exacting employer, and had treated the
young man, whom everybody else loved and esteemed,
with the greatest rigor; a course which had not increased
his popularity. The method of election was for the
candidates to step out of the ranks, when the electors
advanced and joined the man whom they chose to lead
them. Three-fourths of the company at once went to
Lincoln; and when it was seen how strongly the tide
was set in his favor, the friends of the rival candidate deserted him, one after another, until he was left
standing almost alone. He was unspeakably mortified
and disappointed, while Lincoln's joy was proportionably
great.

The latter served three months in the Black Hawk
war, and made acquaintance with the usual campaign-
ing experiences, but was in no battle. He still owns
the lands in Iowa that he located with warrants for service performed in the war.

An incident of the campaign, in which Lincoln is

* "William Kirkpatrick" — I never
worked for him — L.

concerned,* illustrates a trait of his character no less
prominent than his qualities of integrity and truth.
One day an old Indian wandered into Lincoln's camp,
and was instantly seized by his men. The general
opinion was that he ought to be put to death. They
were in the field for the purpose of killing Indians, and
to spare the slaughter of one that Providence had delivered into their hands was something of which these
honest pioneers could not abide the thought. It was
to little purpose that the wretched aborigine showed a
letter signed by General Cass, and certifying him to be
not only a model of all the savage virtues, but a sincere
friend of the whites. He was about to be sacrificed,
when Lincoln boldly declared that the sacrifice should
not take place. He was at once accused of cowardice,
and of a desire to conciliate the Indians. Nevertheless,
he stood firm, proclaiming that even barbarians would not
kill a helpless prisoner. If any one thought him a cow-
ard, let him step out and be satisfied of his mistake, in
any way he chose. As to this poor old Indian, he had
no doubt he was all that the letter of General Cass
affirmed; he declared that they should kill him before
they touched the prisoner. His argument, in fine, was
so convincing, and his manner so determined, that the
copper-colored ally of the whites was suffered to go
his ways, and departed out of the hostile camp of his
friends unhurt.

* The authority for this anecdote is Mr. William G. Green, a tried and inti-
mate friend of Lincoln during early manhood.

After his return from the wars, Lincoln determined to
test the strength of his popularity, by offering himself
as a candidate for the Legislature. Added to the good-
will which had carried him into the captaincy, he had
achieved a warmer place in the hearts of those who had
followed his fortunes during the war, by his bravery, social qualities, and uprightness. He was warm-hearted and
good-natured, and told his stories, of which he had numbers, in better style than any other man in the camp. No
one was so fleet of foot; and in those wrestlings which
daily enlivened the tedium of camp life, he was never
thrown but once, and then by a man of superior science
who was not his equal in strength. These were qualities
which commended him to the people, and made him the
favorite officer of the battalion.

Parties, at this time, were distinguished as Adams
parties and Jackson parties, and in Lincoln's county the
Jackson men were vastly in the ascendant. He was a
stanch Adams man, and, being comparatively unknown
in the remoter parts of the county, was defeated. In his
own neighborhood the vote was almost unanimous in his
favor; though he had only arrived from the war and
announced himself as a candidate ten days before the
election. Indeed, he received, at this election, one
more vote in his precinct than both of the rival candidates for Congress together.*

---

* The following is the vote taken from the poll-book in Springfield: For
Congress—Jonathan H. Pugh, 179, and Joseph Duncan, 97. For Legislature—
Lincoln, 277.

Defeated, but far from dismayed, Lincoln once more turned his attention to business. He was still poor, for though thrifty enough, he never could withstand the appeals of distress, nor sometimes refuse to become security for those who asked the use of his name. His first surveying had been done with a grape-vine instead of a chain, and having indorsed a note which was not paid, his compass was seized and sold. One James Short bought it and returned it to Lincoln. The surveyor of Sangamon county, John Calhoun, (since notorious for his candle-box concealment of the election returns in Kansas,) deputed to Lincoln that part of the county in which he resided, and he now assumed the active practice of surveying, and continued to live upon the slender fees of his office until 1834, when he was elected to the Legislature by the largest vote cast for any candidate.

Before this election Lincoln had engaged and failed in merchandising on his own account.

It is supposed that it was at New Salem that Lincoln, while a "clerk" in Offutt's store, first saw Stephen A. Douglas, and, probably, the acquaintance was renewed during Lincoln's proprietorship of the store which he afterward bought in the same place.*

* Lincoln expressly stated, in reply to some badinage of Douglas, during the debates of 1858, that he never kept a grocery anywhere. Out West, a grocery is understood to be a place where the chief article of commerce is whisky. Lincoln's establishment was, in the Western sense, a store; that is, he sold tea, coffee, sugar, powder, lead, and other luxuries and necessaries of pioneer existence. Very possibly his store was not without the "elixir of life," with which nearly everybody renewed the flower of youth in those days; though this is not a matter of absolute history, nor perhaps of vital consequence.

4

One Reuben Radford was Lincoln's predecessor. He had fallen, by some means, into disfavor with Clary's Grove Boys, who, one evening, took occasion to break in the windows of his establishment. Reuben was discouraged. Perhaps it would not be going too far to allude to his situation as discouraging. At any rate, he told a young farmer,* who came to trade with him the next day, that he was going to close out his business. What would Mr. Green give him for his stock? Mr. Green looked about him and replied, only half in earnest, Four hundred dollars. The offer was instantly accepted, and the business transferred to Mr. Green. On the following day Lincoln chanced to come in, and being informed of the transaction, proposed that he and Green should invoice the stock, and see how much he had made. They found that it was worth about six hundred dollars, and Lincoln gave Mr. Green a hundred and twenty-five dollars for his bargain, while Green indorsed the notes of Lincoln and one Berry, to Radford for the remaining four hundred. Berry was a thriftless soul, it seems, and after a while the store fell into a chronic decay, and, in the idiom of the region, finally *winked out.*

Lincoln was moneyless, having previously invested his whole fortune in a surveyor's compass and books, and Berry was uncertain. Young Green was compelled to pay the notes given to Radford. He afterward removed to Tennessee, where he married, and was living

---

* Mr. W. T. Green, now one of the most influential and wealthy men of his part of Illinois.

in forgetfulness of his transaction with Lincoln, when he one day received a letter from that person, stating he was now able to pay back to Green the amount for which he had indorsed. Lincoln was by this time in the practice of the law, and it was with the first earnings of his profession, that he discharged this debt, principal and interest.

The moral need not be insisted on, and this instance is not out of the order of Abraham Lincoln's whole life. That the old neighbors and friends of such a man should regard him with an affection and faith little short of man-worship, is the logical result of a life singularly pure, and an integrity without flaw.

CHAPTER IV.

IT is seen that Abraham Lincoln was first elected to a seat in the Legislature, in 1834, in the face of the unpopularity of his political principles, by a larger vote than that given to any other candidate. As a legislator he served his constituents so well that he was three times afterward returned to his place; in 1836, in 1838, and in 1840. He then terminated his legislative career by a positive refusal to be again a candidate.

The period embraced by the eight years in which Lincoln represented Sangamon county, was one of the greatest material activity in Illinois. So early as 1820, the young State was seized with the "generous rage" for public internal improvements, then prevalent in New York, Pennsylvania, and Ohio, and in its sessions for a score of succeeding years, the Legislature was occupied by the discussion of various schemes for enhancing the prosperity of the State. The large canal uniting the waters of Lake Michigan and the Illinois river was completed at a cost of more than eight millions. By a Board of Commissioners of Public Works, specially created, provisions were made for expensive improvements of the rivers Wabash, Illinois, Rock, Kaskaskia, and Little Wabash, and the great Western mail route from

(44)

Vincennes to St. Louis. Under the charge of the same Board, six railroads connecting principal points were projected, and appropriations made for their completion at an immense outlay.

One effect of a policy so wild and extravagant was to sink the State in debt. Another was to attract vast immigration, and fill up her broad prairies with settlers. Individuals were ruined; the corporate State became embarrassed; but benefits have resulted in a far greater degree than could have been hoped when the crash first came. It is not yet time to estimate the ultimate good to be derived from these improvements, though the immediate evil has been tangible enough.

The name of Abraham Lincoln is not found recorded in favor of the more visionary of these schemes; but he has always favored public improvements, and his voice was for whatever project seemed feasible and practical. During his first term of service, he was a member of the Committee on Public Accounts and Expenditures. He voted for a bill to incorporate agricultural societies; for the improvement of public roads; for the incorporation of various institutions of learning; for the construction of the Illinois and Michigan Canal; he always fostered the interests of public education, and favored low salaries for public officials. In whatever pertained to the local benefit of his own county, he was active and careful; but his record on this subject is of little interest to the general reader.

Lincoln's voice was ever for measures that relieved

the struggling poor man from pecuniary or political difficulties; he had himself experienced these difficulties. He therefore supported resolutions for the removal of the property qualification in franchise, and for the granting of pre-emption rights to settlers on the public lands. He was the author of a measure permitting Revolutionary pensioners to loan their pension money without taxation. He advocated a bill exempting from execution Bibles, school-books, and mechanics' tools.

His first recorded vote against Stephen A. Douglas, was on the election of that politician to the Attorney-Generalship by the Legislature.

He twice voted for the Whig candidates for the United States Senate. Otherwise than in the election of Senators, State Legislatures were not then occupied with national affairs, and it is difficult to find anything in Mr. Lincoln's legislative history which is of great national interest. There were no exciting questions, and Mr. Lincoln's speeches were few and brief.* He was twice the candidate (in 1838 and 1840) of the Whig minority for Speaker of the House.

In 1836, when Lincoln was first re-elected to the Legislature, Sangamon county, then of greater geographical mportance than now, was represented by nine members,

---

* A protest from Mr. Lincoln appears on the Journal of the House, in regard to some resolutions which had passed. In this protest he pronounces distinctly against slavery, and takes the first public step toward what is now Republican doctrine.

no one of whom was less than six feet in height—several of them considerably exceeding that altitude. This immensity of stature attracted attention, and the Sangamon members were at once nicknamed *The Long-Nine.* They were genial, hearty-humored fellows, famous whittlers, and distinguished spinners of yarns. They all boarded at the same place, and being of gregarious habits, spent their evenings together. Lincoln was the favorite of the circle; admired for his gift of storytelling, and highly esteemed for his excellent qualities of head and heart, his intellectual shrewdness, his reliability, his good-nature, and generosity. The Illinois Legislature then held its sessions at Vandalia, and Lincoln used to perform his journeys between New Salem and the seat of government on foot, though the remaining eight of the Long-Nine traveled on horseback.

A pleasant story connected with this part of his political career is related by Hon. John D. Stuart. Lincoln and Stuart were both candidates for the Legislature in 1834. Stuart's election was conceded, while that of Lincoln was thought to be comparatively uncertain. The two candidates happened to be present together at a backwoods frolic, when some disaffected of Stuart's party took Lincoln aside, and offered to withdraw votes enough from Stuart to elect him. He rejected the proposal, and at once disclosed the scheme to Stuart, declaring that he would not make such a bargain for any office.

It is by such manly and generous acts that Lincoln has endeared himself to all his old neighbors. It may

be said of him without extravagance that he is beloved
of all—even by those against whose interests he has
conscientiously acted. When in the practice of the law
he was never known to undertake a cause which he believed founded in wrong and injustice. "You are not
strictly in the right," he said to a person who once
wished him to bring a certain suit, and who now tells
the story with profound admiration. "I might give
the other parties considerable trouble, and perhaps beat
them at law, but there would be no justice in it. I am
sorry—I can not undertake your case." "I never knew
Lincoln to do a mean act in his life," said Stuart, the
veteran lawyer, who first encouraged Lincoln to adopt
his profession. "God never made a finer man," ex-
claimed the old backwoods-man, Close, when applied to
for reminiscences of Lincoln. So by the testimony of
all, and in the memory of every one who has known him,
Lincoln is a pure, candid, and upright man, unblem-
ished by those vices which so often disfigure greatness,
utterly incapable of falsehood, and without one base or
sordid trait.

During the Legislative canvass of 1834, John D.
Stuart advised Lincoln to study law, and after the
election he borrowed some of Stuart's books, and began
to read. Other warm and influential friends, (Wm. But-
ler, the present Treasurer of State in Illinois, was one
of these,) came to Lincoln's material aid and encouragement, and assisted him to retrieve his early errors
of generosity. With the support of these friends—for

Lincoln is a man who could receive benefits as nobly as he conferred them—and the slender revenues of his surveyorship, he struggled through the term of his law studies, and was admitted to the bar in 1836.   Business flowed in upon him, and quitting New Salem, he took up his residence at Springfield, where he united his professional fortunes with those of Major Stuart.   The two old friends remained in partnership until Stuart's election to Congress, by which time Lincoln had elevated himself to a position among the first lawyers of the place. In the midst of affairs, however, he never relaxed his habits of study; taking up, one by one, the natural sciences, and thoroughly acquainting himself with the abstrusest metaphysics.   He remains to this day a severe and indefatigable student—never suffering any subject to which he directs his attention, to pass without profound investigation.

5

CHAPTER V.

WE now find Abraham Lincoln beginning to assume an active part in the political affairs of Illinois.

He is known to the Whigs throughout the State, and his general popularity is as great as the esteem and regard in which he is held by those personally acquainted with him.

The talented young Whig has founded his reputation upon qualities that make every man proud to say he is the friend of Lincoln.

No admirer, who speaks in his praise, must pause to conceal a stain upon his good name. No true man falters in his affection at the remembrance of any mean action or littleness in the life of Lincoln.

The purity of his reputation, the greatness and dignity of his ambition, ennoble every incident of his career, and give significance to all the events of his past.

It is true that simply to have mauled rails, and commanded a flat-boat, is not to have performed splendid actions. But the fact that Lincoln has done these things, and has risen above them by his own force, confers a dignity upon them; and the rustic boy, who is to be President in 1900, may well be consoled and encouraged in his labors when he recalls these incidents in the history of one whose future once wore no brighter aspect than his own wears now.

The emigrant, at the head of the slow oxen that drag his household gods toward the setting sun—toward some Illinois yet further west—will take heart and hope when he remembers that Lincoln made no prouder entrance into the State of which he is now the first citizen.

The young student, climbing unaided up the steep ascent—he who has begun the journey after the best hours of the morning are lost forever—shall not be without encouragement when he finds the footprints of another in the most toilsome windings of his path.

Lincoln's future success or unsuccess can affect nothing in the past. The grandeur of his triumph over all the obstacles of fortune, will remain the same. Office can not confer honors brighter than those he has already achieved ; it is the Presidency, not a great man, that is elevated, if such be chosen chief magistrate.

We have seen that, in 1842, he declines re-election to the State Legislature, after eight years' service in that body. He has already been on the Harrison electoral ticket, and has distinguished himself in the famous canvass of 1840.

But it is not as a politician alone, that Lincoln is heard of at this time. After Stuart's election to Congress has dissolved their connection, Lincoln forms a partnership with Judge Logan, one of the first in his profession at Springfield, and continues the practice of the law, with rising repute.

His characteristics as an advocate, are an earnestness and sincerity of manner, and a directness, conciseness, and strength of style; he appeals, at other times, to the weapons of good-humored ridicule as ably as to the heavier arms of forensic combat. He is strongest in civil cases, but in a criminal cause that enlists his sympathy he is also great. It is then that the advocate's convictions, presented to the jury in terse and forcible, yet eloquent language, sometimes outweigh the charge of the judge. Juries listen to him, and concur in his arguments; for his known truth has preceded his arguments, and he triumphs. There may be law and evidence against him, but the belief that Lincoln is *right*, nothing can shake in the minds of those who know the man.

He prepares his cases with infinite care, when he has nothing but technical work before him. The smallest detail of the affair does not escape him. All the parts are perfectly fitted together, and the peculiar powers of his keen, analytic mind are brought into full play. He has not the quickness which characterizes Douglas, and which is so useful to the man who adventures in law or politics. But he is sufficiently alert, and recovers himself in time to achieve success.

Lincoln does not grow rich at the law, and has not grown rich to this day, though possessing a decent competence, and owing no man anything. Poor men, who have the misfortune to do with courts, come to Lincoln, who has never been known to exact an exorbitant fee, and whose demands are always proportioned to their poverty. There is record of a case which he gained for a young mechanic, after carrying it through three courts, and of his refusal to receive more than a comparative trifle in return.

Meantime, in the year 1842, Lincoln married a woman worthy to be the companion of his progress toward honor and distinction. Miss Mary Todd, who became his wife, is the daughter of Robert Todd, of Lexington, Kentucky, a man well known in that State, and formerly the clerk of the lower House of Congress. At the time of her marriage, Miss Todd was the belle of Springfield society—accomplished and intellectual, and possessing all the social graces native in the women of Kentucky.*

If, at this point of his career, Lincoln looked back over his past life with proud satisfaction, his feeling was one in which every reader, who has traced his history, must sympathize.

It was hardly more than a half-score of years since he had entered Illinois, driving an ox-wagon, laden with the " plunder " of a backwoods emigrant. He was utterly unknown, and without friends who could advance him in any way. He was uneducated, and almost unlettered.

In ten years he had reversed all the relations of his

---

* Three living sons are the children of this marriage; the first of whom was born in 1843, the second in 1850, and the third in 1853. Another son, who was born in 1846, is now dead.

life. No man had now more friends among all classes of people. No man among his neighbors had a wider intelligence, or more eager and comprehensive mind. No man of his age stood better in his profession, or in politics. No one was in a fairer road to happiness and success. And all this had been accomplished through his own exertion, and the favor which his many noble traits awakened in those around him.

He might well exult in view of all that had been, and all that was.

But, however this may have been, Lincoln did not pause to exult. He exulted in full career; for already the great battle of 1844 was approaching, and he was to take a prominent part in the contest. Many of the people of Illinois have distinct recollection of the brilliant debates which he conducted with Calhoun and Thomas, and these are loth to concede that they have ever been surpassed. The debaters met in all the principal cities and towns of that State, and afterward carried the war into Indiana.

It may be supposed that the fortunes of the war varied, but there are popular stories related of these encounters that give rather amusing results of one of Lincoln's frequent successes.

The contest turned upon the annexation of Texas, to which measure Lincoln was opposed, in proportion as he loved and honored Henry Clay. It has been said that no man ever had such friends as Clay possessed. It may be said that he never possessed a friend more

ardent, attached, and faithful than Abraham Lincoln.
Throughout that disastrous campaign of 1844, Lincoln
was a zealous and indefatigable soldier in the Whig
cause.   His name was on the electoral ticket of Illinois,
and he shared the defeat of his gallant leader—a defeat
which precipitated the Mexican war, with its attendant
evils, and the long train of dissensions, discords, and
pro-slavery aggressions which have followed.

In the lull which comes after a Presidential battle,
Lincoln, while mingling in State politics, devoted himself more particularly to professional affairs, though he
continued an enemy to the Mexican war, and his election
to Congress in 1846, took place in full view of this en-
mity.   It is worthy of note, in this connection, that he
was the only Whig elected in Illinois at that time.

CHAPTER VI.

THE period over which Lincoln's Congressional career extends, is one of the most interesting of our history.

Mr. Polk's favorite scheme of a war of glory and aggrandizement, had been in full course of unsatisfactory experiment. Our little army in Mexico had conquered a peace as rapidly as possible. The battles of Palo Alto, Reseca de la Palma, Monterey, Buena Vista, Cerro Gordo, and the rest, had been fought to the triumph and honor of the American arms. Everywhere, the people had regarded these successes with patriotic pride. They had felt a yet deeper interest in them because the volunteer system had taken the war out of the hands of mercenaries, and made it, in some sort, the crusade of Anglo-Saxon civilization and vigor against the semi-barbarism and effeteness of the Mexican and Spanish races.

Yet, notwithstanding the popular character thus given to the army, the war itself had not increased in popularity. People, in their sober second thought, rejected the specious creed, "Our country, right or wrong," and many looked forward earnestly and anxiously to a conclusion of hostilities.

The elections of Congressmen had taken place, and in

the Thirtieth Congress, which assembled on the 6th of December, 1847, the people, by a majority of seven Whigs in the House, pronounced against the war, though hardly more than a year had elapsed since their Representatives, by a vote of one hundred and twenty-two to fourteen, had declared war to exist through the act of Mexico.

In those days, great men shaped the destinies of the nation. In the Senate sat Clay, Calhoun, Benton, Webster, Corwin. In the House were Palfrey, Winthrop, Wilmot, Giddings, Adams.

The new member from Illinois, who had distinguished himself in 1844 as the friend of Clay and the enemy of Texan annexation, took his seat among these great men as a representative of the purest Whig principles; he was opposed to the war, as Corwin was; he was anti-slavery, as Clay was; he favored internal improvements, as all the great Whigs did.

And as Abraham Lincoln never sat astride of any fence, unless in his rail-splitting days; as water was never carried on both of his square shoulders; as his prayers to Heaven have never been made with reference to a compromise with other powers; so, throughout his Congressional career, you find him the bold advocate of the principles which he believed to be right. He never dodged a vote. He never minced matters with his opponents. He had not been fifteen days in the House when he made known what manner of man he was.

On the 22d of December he offered a series of reso-

lutions,* making the most damaging inquiries of the
President, as to the verity of certain statements in his
messages of May and December.   Mr. Polk had represented that the Mexicans were the first aggressors in the

---

* The following are the resolutions, which it is judged best to print here in
full :

" *Whereas*, the President of the United States, in his Message of May 11,
1846, has declared that ' the Mexican government refused to receive him, [the
envoy of the United States,] or listen to his propositions, but, after a long-con-
tinued series of menaces, have at last invaded *our territory*, and shed the blood of
our fellow-citizens on *our own soil*.'

" And again, in his Message of December 8, 1846, that 'we had ample cause of
war against Mexico long before the breaking out of hostilities ; but even then
we forbore to take redress into our own hands, until Mexico basely became the
aggressor, by invading *our soil* in hostile array, and shedding the blood of our
citizens.'

" And yet again, in his Message of December 7, 1847, ' The Mexican government refused even to hear the terms of adjustment which he (our minister of
peace) was authorized to propose, and finally, under wholly unjustifiable pre-
texts, involved the two countries in war, by invading the territory of the State
of Texas, striking the first blow, and shedding the blood of our citizens on *our
own soil*.'

" And whereas this House is desirous to obtain a full knowledge of all the
facts which go to establish whether the particular spot on which the blood of
our citizens was so shed, was, or was not, at that time; *our own soil*.   Therefore,

" *Resolved, by the House of Representatives*, That the President of the United
States be respectfully requested to inform this House—

" 1st. Whether the spot on which the blood of our citizens was shed, as in his
memorial declared, was, or was not within the territory of Spain, at least, after
the treaty of 1819, until the Mexican revolution.

" 2d. Whether that spot is, or is not within the territory which was wrested
from Spain by the revolutionary government of Mexico.

" 3d. Whether that spot is, or is not within a settlement of people, which settlement has existed ever since long before the Texas Revolution, and until its
inhabitants fled before the approach of the United States army.

" 4th. Whether that settlement is, or is not isolated from any and all other
settlements of the Gulf and the Rio Grande on the south and west, and of wide
uninhabited regions on the north and east.

" 5th. Whether the people of that settlement, or a majority of them, have
ever submitted themselves to the government or laws of Texas, or of the United
States, of consent or of compulsion, either of accepting office or voting at elections, or paying taxes, or serving on juries, or having process served on them
or in any other way.

" 6th. Whether the people of that settlement did or did not flee at the ap-

existing hostilities, by an invasion of American soil, and
an effusion of American blood, after rejecting the friendly overtures made by this country.

Mr. Lincoln's resolutions demanded to know whether
the spot on which American blood had been shed, was
not Mexican, or at least, disputed territory; whether the
Mexicans who shed this blood had not been driven from
their homes by the approach of our arms; whether the
Americans killed were not armed soldiers sent into
Mexican territory, by order of the President of the
United States.

Parliamentary strategy defeated the proposed inquiry,
the resolutions going over under the rules.

On the 12th of January, Mr. Lincoln made a speech*
on the reference of different parts of the President's
message. In this speech he justified a previous vote of
sentiment, declaring that the war had been " unnecessa-
rily and unconstitutionally commenced by the President
of the United States." That vote had been pressed
upon the opposition of the House, by the President's

---

proaching of the United States army, leaving unprotected their homes and their
growing crops *before* the blood was shed, as in the message stated; and whether
the first blood so shed was, or was not shed within the inclosure of one of the
people who had thus fled from it.

"7th. Whether our *citizens* whose blood was shed, as in his message declared,
were, or were not, at that time, armed officers and soldiers sent into that settlement by the military order of the President, through the Secretary of War.

" 8th. Whether the military force of the United States was, or was not so sent
into that settlement after General Taylor had more than once intimated to the
War Department that, in his opinion, no such movement was necessary to the
defense or protection of Texas."—*Congressional Globe*, vol. xviii, 1st session, 30th
Congress, page 64.

* *Globe* Appendix, vol, xix, page 93.

friends, in order to force an expression of opinion which should seem unjust to that functionary. Discussing this point, Mr. Lincoln coolly argued to conclusions the most injurious to the administration ; showing that even though the President had attempted to construe a vote of supplies for the army into a vote applauding his official course, the opposition had remained silent, until Mr. Polk's friends forced this matter upon them. Mr. Lincoln then took up the arguments of the President's message, one by one, and exposed their fallacy ; and following the line of inquiry marked out by his resolutions of December, proved that the first American blood shed by Mexicans, was in retaliation for injuries received from us, and that hostilities had commenced on Mexican soil. The speech was characterized by all the excellences of Lincoln's later style—boldness, trenchant logic, and dry humor.

He next appears in the debates,* as briefly advocating a measure to give bounty lands to the surviving volunteer soldiers of the war of 1812, and arguing the propriety of permitting all soldiers holding land warrants, to locate their lands in different parcels, instead of requiring the location to be made in one body.

As Lincoln is a man who never talks unless he has something particular to say, (rare and inestimable virtue !) a period of some three months elapsed before he made another speech in Congress. On the 20th of June,

---

1848, the Civil and Diplomatic Appropriation bill being under consideration, he addressed to the House and the country, a clear and solid argument in favor of the improvement of rivers and harbors.*   As a Western man, and as a man whom his own boating experiences had furnished with actual knowledge of the perils of snags and sawyers, he had always been in favor of a measure which commended itself at once to the heart and the pocket of the West.   As the representative of a State with many hundred miles of Mississippi river, and vast river interests, he argued to show that an enlightened system of internal improvements, must be of national as well as local benefit.†   The prevailing Democratic errors on this subject, as Mr. Lincoln succinctly stated them, were as follows:

" That internal improvements ought not to be made by the General Government:

" 1. Because they would overwhelm the Treasury.

" 2. Because, while their *burdens* would be general, their *benefits* would be *local* and *partial*, involving an obnoxious inequality; and,

" 3. Because they would be unconstitutional.

" 4. Because the States may do enough by the levy and collection of tonnage duties; or, if not,

" 5. That the Constitution may be amended.

Globe Appendix, vol. xix, page 709.

† This speech will be found printed at length in the appendix to the present biography.

'The sum," said Lincoln, "of these positions is, Do nothing at all, lest you do something wrong."

He then proceeded to assail each of the positions, demolishing them one after another. That admirable simplicity of diction which dashes straight at the heart of a subject, and that singular good sense which teaches a man to stop when he is done, are no less the characteristics of this effort than of all the other speeches of Mr. Lincoln.

Of a different manner, but illustrating a phase of his mind equally marked, is the speech he made in the House on the 27th of July,* when he discussed the political questions of the day with reference to the Presidential contest between General Taylor and Mr. Cass. It abounds in broad ridicule and broad drollery—the most effective and the most good-natured. Severe and sarcastic enough, when treating a false principle, it seems never to have been one of Lincoln's traits to indulge in bitter personalities. His only enemies, therefore, are those who hate his principles.

On the 21st of December, 1848, Mr. Gott, of New York, offered a resolution in the House, instructing the Committee on the District of Columbia to report a bill for the abolition of the slave-trade in that District. There were men in Congress then who had not forgotten the traditions of the Republican fathers, and who were indignant that slaves should be bought and sold

---

* *Globe Appendix*, vol. xix, page 1041.

in the shadow of the capital—that the slave-trader should make the political metropolis of the Republic a depot on the line of his abominable traffic.

As soon as the resolution of Mr. Gott was read, a motion was made to lay it on the table, which was lost by a vote of eighty-one to eighty-five. A hot struggle ensued; but the resolution was adopted. An immediate attempt to reconsider proved ineffectual. The action upon reconsideration was postponed from day to day, until the 10th of January following, when Mr. Lincoln proposed that the committee should be instructed to report a bill forbidding the sale, beyond the District of Columbia, of any slave born within its limits, or the removal of slaves from the District, except such servants as were in attendance upon their masters temporarily residing at Washington; establishing an apprenticeship of twenty-one years for all slaves born within the District subsequent to the year 1850; providing for their emancipation at the expiration of the apprenticeship; authorizing the United States to buy and emancipate all slaves within the District, whose owners should desire to set them free in that manner; finally submitting the bill to a vote of the citizens of the District for approval.

It is well known that the efforts to abolish the slave-trade in the District of Columbia have resulted in nothing.* The wise, humane, and temperate measure of Mr. Lincoln shared the fate of all the rest.

* Mr. Lincoln's preposition had received the approval of Mayor Seaton, of Washington, who informed him that it would meet the approbation of the

Another great measure of the Congress in which Mr. Lincoln figured, was the Wilmot Proviso—now a favorite Republican measure—and so pervading, with its distinctive principle (opposition to slavery extension) the whole Republican soul, that, whether in or out of platforms, it remains the life and strength of the party. To this measure Mr. Lincoln was fully committed. Indeed, it is a peculiarity of this man, that he has *always* acted decidedly one way or the other. He thought the Mexican war wrong. He opposed it with his whole heart and strength. He thought the Wilmot Proviso right, and he says he " had the pleasure of voting for it, in one way or another, *about forty times."*

Mr. Lincoln was one of those who advocated the nomination of General Taylor, in the National Whig Convention of 1848. Returning to Illinois after the adjournment of Congress, he took the stump for his favorite candidate, and was active throughout that famous canvass. In 1849, he retired from Congress, firmly declining re-nomination, and resumed the practice of' his profession.

The position which he maintained in the House of Representatives was eminently respectable. His name appears oftener in the ayes and noes, than in the debates; he spoke therefore with the more force and effect when he felt called upon to express his opinion.

---

leading citizens. Afterward, Southern Congressmen visited the Mayor and persuaded him to withdraw the moral support given to the measure. When this had been done, the chief hope of success was destroyed, and the bill, of which Mr. Lincoln gave notice, was never introduced.

The impression that his Congressional speeches give you, is the same left by all others that he has made. You feel that he has not argued to gain a point, but to show the truth ; that it is not Lincoln he wishes to sustain, but Lincoln's principles.

6

CHAPTER VII.

PEACE to the old Whig party, which is dead! When a man has ceased to live, we are cheaply magnanimous in the exaltation of his virtues, and we repair whatever wrong we did him when alive by remorselessly abusing every one who hints that he may have been an imperceptible trifle lower than the angels.

It is with such post-mortem greatness of soul that the leaders of the Democracy have cherished the memory of the Whig party, and gone about the stump, clad in moral sackcloth and craped hats.

If you will believe these stricken mourners, virtue went out with that lamented organization; and there is but one true man unhanged in America, and he is a stoutish giant, somewhat under the middle size.

In speaking, therefore, of the Whig party, you have first to avoid offense to the gentlemen who reviled its great men in their lifetime, and who have a fondness for throwing the honored dust of the past into the eyes of the present. Then, respect is due to the feelings of those Republicans who abandoned the Whig party only after the last consolations of religion had been administered, and who still remember it with sincere regret.

The prejudices of another class of our friends must

(66)

be treated with decent regard. Very many old Democrats in the Republican ranks are earnestly persuaded that in former times they were right in their opposition to the Whigs.

Yet one more variety of opinion must be consulted— the opinion that the Whig party had survived its usefulness, and that all which was good in it has now entered upon a higher and purer state of existence in the Republican organization.

Doubtless it would be better not to mention the Whig party at all. Unfortunately for the ends of strict prudence, the story of Abraham Lincoln's life involves allusion to it, since he was once a Whig, and became a Republican, and not a Democrat. But as every Republican is a code of by-laws unto himself—subject only to the Chicago platform—perhaps we may venture to reverently speak of the shade which still, it is said, revisits the glimpses of Boston; and to recount the events which preceded its becoming a shade.

So early as 1848 the dismemberment of the Whig party commenced. It had been distinguished by many of the characteristics of the Republican party, among which is the reserved right of each member of the organization to think and act for himself, on his own responsibility, as already intimated. Whenever its leaders deflected from the straight line of principle, their followers called them to account; and a persistence in the advocacy of measures repugnant to the individual sense of right, caused disaffection.

Many sincere and earnest men, who supported Henry Clay with ardor, ceased to be Whigs when General Taylor was nominated, because they conceived that his nomination was a departure from the Clay Whig principles of opposition to the Mexican war and the acquisition of slave territory.

This is not the place to pronounce upon the wisdom or justice of their course. Others, as sincere and earnest as they, supported General Taylor, and continued to act with the Whig party throughout the Fillmore administration.

The assimilation of the two great parties on the slavery question in 1852, widened the distance between the Whigs and the Free Soilers, and the former were, in the opinion of the latter, demoralized before the election in which they suffered so total an overthrow, though they continued steadfast in their devotion to the Whig name until 1854, when the first organization of the Republicans took place, under the name of the Anti-Nebraska party.

The Whig Free Soilers were eager and glad to fraternize with their old friends; and all greeted with enthusiasm the vast accessions which the new party received from the men who had given spiritual vitality to the Democracy.

Those members of both the old parties, who were particularly sensible to the attractions of office, those whom no pro-slavery aggression could render superior to the luxury of a feeble or selfish acquiescence, also coalesced, and now constitute, with a few sincere political reminiscences, the Democracy of the North.

Up to the time of the repeal of the Missouri Compromise, Abraham Lincoln remained a Whig, both from conviction and affection.

In 1848, he had made speeches in favor of the election of General Taylor, in Maryland, in Massachusetts, and in Illinois.   In his own Congressional district, where his word has always been platform enough, the success of his canvass was declared by a majority of fifteen hundred for Taylor.

After his retirement from Congress, he devoted himself, with greater earnestness than ever before, to the duties of his profession, and extended his business and repute.   He did not reappear in the political arena until 1852, when his name was placed on the Scott electoral ticket.

In the canvass of that year, so disastrous to the Whig party throughout the country, Lincoln appeared several times before the people of his State as the advocate of Scott's claims for the Presidency.   But the prospect was everywhere so disheartening, and in Illinois the cause was so utterly desperate, that the energies of the Whigs were paralyzed, and Lincoln did less in this Presidential struggle than any in which he had ever engaged.

During that lethargy which preceded the dissolution of his party, he had almost relinquished political aspirations.   Successful in his profession, happy in his home, secure in the affection of his neighbors, with books, competence, and leisure—ambition could not tempt him. It required the more thrilling voice of danger to freedom, to call the veteran of so many good fights into the field. The call was made.

It would be useless to recount here the history of the Missouri Compromise, and the circumstances attending the violation of that compact, though that history is properly a part of the biography of every public man in the country. Throughout the fierce contest which preceded the repeal of the Compromise, and the storm of indignation which followed that repeal, the whole story was brought vividly before the people, and can not now have faded from their recollection. Those to whom it is yet strange, will find it briefly and faithfully related in the speech of Abraham Lincoln, made in reply to Douglas, at Peoria, in October, 1854.*

---

* Printed in full in this volume. Douglas and Lincoln had previously met at Springfield, where the latter played David to the abbreviated Goliah of the former. The following spirited sketch of the scene is by the editor of the Chicago *Press and Tribune*, who was present :

"The affair came off on the fourth day of October, 1854. The State Fair had been in progress two days, and the capital was full of all manner of men. The Nebraska bill had been passed on the previous twenty-second of May. Mr. Douglas had returned to Illinois to meet an outraged constituency. He had made a fragmentary speech in Chicago, the people filling up each hiatus in a peculiar and good-humored way. He called the people a mob—they called him a rowdy. The 'mob' had the best of it, both then and at the election which succeeded. The notoriety of all these events had stirred up the politics of the State from bottom to top. Hundreds of politicians had met at Springfield, expecting a tournament of an unusual character—Douglas, Breese, Koerner, Lincoln, Trumbull, Matteson, Yates, Codding, John Calhoun, (of the order of the candle-box,) John M. Palmer, the whole house of the McConnells, Singleton, (known to fame in the Mormon war,) Thomas L. Harris, and a host of others. Several speeches were made before, and several after, the passage between Lincoln and Douglas, but that was justly held to be *the* event of the season.

"We do not remember whether a challenge to debate passed between the

The people were glad to hear the voice of their favorite once more, and Lincoln's canvass of Illinois was most triumphant. The legislative elections were held, and those who denounced the repeal of the Missouri Compromise, were found to be in the majority.

---

friends of the speakers or not, but there was a perfectly amicable understanding between Lincoln and Douglas, that the former should speak two or three hours, and the latter reply in just as little or as much time as he chose. Mr. Lincoln took the stand at two o'clock—a large crowd in attendance, and Mr. Douglas seated on a small platform in front of the desk. The first half hour of Mr. Lincoln's speech was taken up with compliments to his distinguished friend Judge Douglas, and dry allusions to the political events of the past few years. His distinguished friend, Judge Douglas, had taken his seat, as solemn as the Cock-Lane ghost, evidently with the design of not moving a muscle till it came his turn to speak. The laughter provoked by Lincoln's exordium, however, soon began to make him uneasy; and when Mr. L. arrived at his (Douglas's) speech, pronouncing the Missouri Compromise 'a sacred thing, which no ruthless hand would ever be reckless enough to disturb,' he opened his lips far enough to remark, 'A first-rate speech!' This was the beginning of an amusing colloquy.

" ' Yes,' continued Mr. Lincoln, 'so affectionate was my friend's regard for this Compromise line, that when Texas was admitted into the Union, and it was found that a strip extended north of 36° 30′, he actually introduced a bill extending the line and prohibiting slavery in the northern edge of the new State.'

" ' And you voted against the bill,' said Douglas.

" ' Precisely so,' replied Lincoln; ' I was in favor of running the line *a great deal further south.*'

" ' About this time,' the speaker continued, ' my distinguished friend introduced me to a particular friend of his, one David Wilmot, of Pennsylvania.' [Laughter.]

" ' I thought,' said Douglas, 'you would find him congenial company.'

" ' So I did,' replied Lincoln. ' I had the pleasure of voting for his proviso, in one way and another, about forty times. It was a *Democratic* measure then, I believe. At any rate, General Cass scolded honest John Davis, of Massachusetts, soundly, for talking away the last hours of the session, so that he (Cass) couldn't crowd it through. *A propos* of General Cass: if I am not greatly mistaken, he has a prior claim to my distinguished friend, to the authorship of Popular Sovereignty. The old general has an infirmity for writing letters. Shortly after the scolding he gave John Davis, he wrote his Nicholson letter'—

" Douglas (solemnly)—' God Almighty placed man on the earth, and told him to choose between good and evil. That was the origin of the Nebraska bill!'

"Lincoln—' Well, the priority of invention being settled, let us award all credit to Judge Douglas for being the first to discover it.'

" It would be impossible, in these limits, to give an idea of the strength of

The election of a United States Senator took place the following winter, and General Shields was superseded. This gentleman, who, listening to the seductive persuasions of his voiceful colleague, was said to have voted for the repeal of the Compromise against his own convictions, was a candidate for re-election. On the part of the opposition majority there were two candidates, Lincoln and Trumbull. The great body of the opposition voted steadily for the former on several ballots; but some Democrats who had been elected on the anti-Nebraska issue, continued to cast their votes for Trumbull.

Lincoln feared that this dissension might result in the election of a less positive man than Trumbull, and with

---

Mr. Lincoln's argument. We deemed it by far the ablest effort of the campaign, from whatever source. The occasion was a great one, and the speaker was every way equal to it. The effect produced on the listeners was magnetic. No one who was present will ever forget the power and vehemence of the following passage:

"My distinguished friend says it is an insult to the emigrants to Kansas and Nebraska to suppose they are not able to govern themselves. We must not slur over an argument of this kind because it happens to tickle the ear. It must be met and answered. I admit that the emigrant to Kansas and Nebraska is competent to govern *himself*, but,' the speaker rising to his full hight, '*I deny his right to govern any other person* WITHOUT THAT PERSON'S CONSENT.' The applause which followed this triumphant refutation of a cunning falsehood, was but an earnest of the victory at the polls which followed just one month from that day.

"When Mr. Lincoln had concluded, Mr. Douglas strode hastily to the stand. As usual, he employed ten minutes in telling how grossly he had been abused. Recollecting himself, he added, 'though in a perfectly courteous manner'— abused in a perfectly courteous manner! He then devoted half an hour to showing that it was indispensably necessary to California emigrants, Santa Fè traders and others, to have organic acts provided for the Territories of Kansas and Nebraska—that being precisely the point which nobody disputed. Having established this premise to his satisfaction, Mr. Douglas launched forth into an argument wholly apart from the positions taken by Mr. Lincoln. He had about half finished at six o'clock, when an adjournment to tea was effected. The speaker insisted strenuously upon his right to resume in the evening, but we believe the second part of that speech has not been delivered to this day.

his usual unselfishness, appealed to his friends to vote
for Trumbull, adjuring them by their friendship to him
to make this concession of individual preference. His
appeal was not in vain, and Trumbull was elected
Senator.

This, however, was not the ~~first~~ sacrifice which he made
to conciliation and union. The ~~anti-Nebraska~~ party of
~~the same year offered~~ him the nomination for Governor;
but in the existing state of organizations, he declined
for the sake of the cause which all had espoused. It
occurs in politics that a force which suddenly rallies
about a principle, may be disheartened by the choice of
a leader whom recent animosities have rendered obnoxious. Lincoln, as a Whig, had been one of the most
decided and powerful opponents of Democracy in Illinois. The period since his opposition to many Democratic members of the anti-Nebraska party had ceased
was very brief, and old feelings of antagonism had not
died away. He perceived that the advancement of himself might impede the advancement of his principles.
Doubtless, he could be elected Governor of Illinois, but
the victory which bore him into office might be less
brilliant and useful than that which could be achieved
under another.   He therefore withdrew his name,
and threw his influence in favor of Governor Bissell,
who had been a Democrat, and who was triumphantly
elected.

It must be remembered that the Republican party ~~had,
as yet, no definite existence~~ in Illinois. The anti-Ne-

7

braska party was the temporary name of the Whigs, Democrats, and Free Soilers, who opposed the repeal of the Missouri Compromise. It is true that a Mass State Convention, with a view to forming a permanent organization, had been held at Springfield, in October; but many anti-Nebraska men, who still adhered to old names, had not taken part in it. The following resolutions were adopted at this Convention:

"1. *Resolved,* That we believe this truth to be self-evident, that when parties become subversive of the ends for which they are established, or incapable of restoring the Government to the true principles of the Constitution, it is the right and duty of the people to dissolve the political bands by which they may have been connected therewith, and to organize new parties upon such principles and with such views as the circumstances and exigencies of the nation may demand.

"2. *Resolved,* That the times imperatively demand the reorganization of parties, and, repudiating all previous party attachments, names, and predilections, we unite ourselves together in defense of the liberty and Constitution of the country, and will hereafter co-operate as the Republican party, pledged to the accomplishment of the following purposes: To bring the administration of the Government back to the control of first principles; to restore Nebraska and Kansas to the position of free territories; that, as the Constitution of the United States vests in the States, and not in Congress, the power to legislate for the extradition of fugitives from labor, to repeal and entirely abrogate the Fugitive Slave law; to restrict slavery to those states in which it exists; to prohibit the admission of any more slave states into the Union; to abolish slavery in the District of Columbia; to exclude slavery from all the territories over which the General Government has exclusive jurisdiction; and to resist the acquirement of any more territories unless the practice of slavery therein forever shall have been prohibited.

"3. *Resolved,* That in furtherance of these principles we will use such Constitutional and lawful means as shall seem best adapted

[handwritten marginalia: Not the resolutions of that convention. Trumper & Galesburg — See debates at Ottawa.]

to their accomplishment, and that we will support no man for office, under the General or State Government, who is not positively and fully committed to the support of these principles, and whose personal character and conduct is not a guarantee that he is reliable, and who shall not have abjured old party allegiance and ties."

In the course of the first debate between Douglas and Lincoln, which was held at Ottawa, in August, 1858, Douglas read these resolutions, declaring that Lincoln had participated in the Convention, and assisted in their adoption. Lincoln met this earliest of a series of misrepresentations with prompt denial, and proved that he was not a member of the Convention.

The actual Republican party of Illinois, dates its formation from a period somewhat later; and Lincoln was one of the first members of the present organization. Not so ultra, probably, as the indignant men who framed the resolutions quoted, he was quite as firmly opposed to slavery. In the speech from which he read, in reply to the charge of Douglas, he gives with Wesleyan point, the reason why indifference to slavery should be abhorred :

"This *declared* indifference, but, as I must think, covert *real* zeal for the spread of slavery, I can not but hate. I hate it because of the monstrous injustice of slavery itself. I hate it because it deprives our republican example of its just influence in the world—enables the enemies of free institutions, with plausibility, to taunt us as hypocrites—causes the real friends of freedom to doubt our sincerity, and especially because it forces so many really good men among ourselves into an open war with the very fundamental principles of civil liberty—criticising the Declaration of Independence, and insisting that there is no right principle of action but *self-interest*."

CHAPTER VIII.

In the Republican National Convention of 1856, Abraham Lincoln received one hundred and two votes for the Vice-Presidential nomination. When the standard-bearers of the party had been selected, he took his rank in the army of freedom, and engaged in the great conflict which followed. The Republicans showed their appreciation of his strength and ability by placing him at the head of their electoral ticket in Illinois; and when in 1858 it was determined to give the Senatorial question the form of a popular contest, by the election of a Legislature pledged to the people, for or against Douglas, Abraham Lincoln was chosen without dissent as the champion of his party.

Much might here be said with regard to his eminent fitness for the conduct of such a canvass; but the result of the election, and his published debates with Douglas, are the best commentary upon his qualifications.

The Republican State ticket of that year was carried by a decisive majority, and the Legislature was lost only through the unfair manner in which the State was districted, and which threw that body into the hands of the Democrats in spite of the popular will.

It may not be improper to allude particularly to cir-

(77)

cumstances connected with the debates between Lincoln and Douglas, which have been so significant in their result, and which have practically made United States Senators in Illinois elective by the people instead of the Legislature.

Lincoln's first great speech of that year was made at Springfield, on the 17th of June, before the State Convention which named him as the Republican candidate for Senator. In this speech he preached the moral conflict, which has always existed and always must exist between the principle of freedom and the principle of slavery; noticed the repeal of the Missouri Compromise, the Dred Scott decision, and the revival of the slave-trade; and with masterly effect exhibited the secret concert with which all the enemies of freedom had acted in their assaults upon our liberties. The speaker concluded with these memorable words, which every Republican should keep in mind, for they have gathered significance in the two years elapsed since their utterance :

"Our cause, then, must be intrusted to, and conducted by, its own undoubted friends—those whose hands are free, whose hearts are in the work—who *do care* for the result. Two years ago the Republicans of the nation mustered over thirteen hundred thousand strong. We did this under the single impulse of resistance to a common danger, with every external circumstance against us. Of strange, discordant, and even hostile elements, we gathered from the four winds, and formed and fought the battle through, under the constant hot fire of a disciplined, proud, and pampered enemy. Did we brave all then, to falter now?—now, when that same enemy is wavering, dissevered, and belligerent? The result is not doubtful. We shall not fail—if we stand firm, we *shall not fail.* Wise counsels may accelerate, or mistakes delay it, but, sooner or later, the victory is sure to come."

The reply made by Douglas to this speech was on the occasion of his reception at Chicago in the July following. Lincoln was present, and spoke in the same city on the next day. Two more great speeches by Douglas, and one more speech by Lincoln were made before they entered the lists in debate.

In one of those speeches, Douglas found occasion—for he was then addressing Lincoln's old friends at Springfield—to pay his tribute to the worth and greatness of his opponent:

"You all know that I am an amiable, good-natured man, and I take great pleasure in bearing testimony to the fact that Mr. Lincoln is a kind-hearted, amiable, good-natured gentleman, with whom no man has a right to pick a quarrel, even if he wanted one. He is a worthy gentleman. I have known him for twenty-five years, and there is no better citizen, and no kinder-hearted man. He is a fine lawyer, possesses high ability, and there is no objection to him, except the monstrous revolutionary doctrines with which he is identified."

On the 24th of July, Lincoln wrote to Douglas proposing the debates which have since become so famous.

Douglas made answer that "recent events had interposed difficulties in the way of such an arrangement," that the Democratic Central Committee had already made appointments for him at different places; but in order to accommodate Mr. Lincoln, he would meet him in seven of the nine Congressional Districts where they had not yet spoken.   He expressed surprise, that if it was Lincoln's original intention to propose these debates, he should have waited until after the plan of the campaign had been arranged by the Democratic Central Committee, before he made known his proposition.

This letter was also written on the 24th of July.   On the 29th Lincoln replied, from Springfield :

" Protesting that your insinuations of attempted unfairness on my part are unjust, and with the hope that you did not very considerately make them, I proceed to reply.   To your statement that ' It has been suggested, recently, that an arrangement had been made to bring out a third candidate for the United States Senate, who, with yourself, should canvass the State in opposition to me,' etc.,* I can only say, that such suggestion must

---

* The following is the statement, in Douglas's letter, alluded to by Lincoln :

" Besides, there is another consideration which should be kept in mind.   It has been suggested, recently, that an arrangement had been made to bring out a third candidate for the United States Senate, who, with yourself, should canvass the State in opposition to me, with no other purpose than to insure my defeat, by dividing the Democratic party for your benefit.   If I should make this arrangement with you, it is more than probable that this other candidate, who has a common object with you, would desire to become a party to it, and claim the right to speak from the same stand ; so that he and you, in concert, might be able to take the opening and closing speech in every case."

have been made by yourself, for certainly none such has been made by or to me, or otherwise, to my knowledge. Surely, you did not *deliberately* conclude, as you insinuate, that I was expecting to draw you into an arrangement of terms, to be agreed on by yourself, by which a third candidate and myself, 'in concert, might be able to take the opening and closing speech in every case.'

"As to your surprise that I did not sooner make the proposal to divide time with you, I can only say, I made it as soon as I resolved to make it. I did not know but that such proposal would come from you; I waited, respectfully, to see. It may have been well known to you that you went to Springfield for the purpose of agreeing on the plan of campaign; but it was not so known to me. When your appointments were announced in the papers, extending only to the 21st of August, I, for the first time, considered it certain that you would make no proposal to me, and then resolved that, if my friends concurred, I would make one to you. As soon thereafter as I could see and consult with friends satisfactorily, I did make the proposal. It did not occur to me that the proposed arrangement could derange your plans after the latest of your appointments already made. After that, there was, before the election, largely over two months of clear time.

" For you to say that we have already spoken at Chicago and Springfield, and that on both occasions I had the concluding speech, is hardly a fair statement. The truth rather is this: At Chicago, July 9th, you made a carefully-prepared conclusion on my speech of June 16th. Twenty four hours after, I made a hasty conclusion on yours of the 9th. You had six days to prepare, and concluded on me again at Bloomington on the 16th. Twenty-four hours after, I concluded again on you at Springfield. In the mean time, you had made another conclusion on me at Springfield, which I did not hear, and of the contents of which I knew nothing when I spoke.; so that your speech made in daylight, and mine at night, of the 17th, at Springfield, were both made in perfect independence of each other. The dates of making all these speeches will show, I think, that in the matter of time for preparation, the advantage has all been on your side; and that none of the external circumstances have stood to my advantage."

Lincoln having left all the arrangements of time, place, and manner of debate to Douglas, the latter made the following proposition, which, (although it allowed Douglas four openings and closes to Lincoln's three, and so gave considerable advantage to him,) Lincoln promptly accepted:

"BEMENT, PIATT Co., ILL., July 30, 1858.

" DEAR SIR:

" Your letter, dated yesterday, accepting my proposition for a joint discussion .at one prominent point in each Congressional District, as stated in my previous letter, was received this morning.

"The times and places designated are as follows :

Ottawa, La Salle county............................August	21st,	1858.
Freeport, Stephenson county...................... "	27th,	"
Jonesboro, Union county.........................September 15th,		"
Charleston, Coles county.......................... "	18th,	"
Galesburgh, Knox county.........................October	7th,	"
Quincy, Adams county.............................. "	13th,	"
Alton, Madison county............................. "	15th,	"

"I agree to your suggestion that we shall alternately open and close the discussion. I will speak at Ottawa one hour, you can reply, occupying an hour and a half, and I will then follow for half an hour. At Freeport, you shall open the discussion and speak one hour; I will follow for an hour and a half, and you can then reply for half an hour. We will alternate in like manner in each successive place.

" Very respectfully, your obedient servant,

"S. A. DOUGLAS.

" Hon. A. LINCOLN, Springfield, Ill."

In the intervals between the debates, which took place as arranged, both speakers addressed audiences separately, and the work on both sides was carried on with unflagging energy.

No one, it seems to me, can read these debates without admiration of Lincoln's ability, courage, and truth, while the impression left by Douglas is that of a great mind bending all its energies to a purpose beneath it ; of an acute logician resorting to sophistry when meeting his opponent's arguments, and to adroit misrepresentation of language and position, when assailing his opinions.

The questions discussed were substantially the same that are at issue now. The spirit of pro-slavery aggression takes many forms, but in nature remains unchanged. Lincoln pursued it through all its disguises, and exposed it at every turn. The subtlest and most audacious champion of slavery that had ever proved false to freedom, was not equal to the conflict. As the pretended advocate of the right of every man to govern himself and regulate his own affairs, Douglas was full of words. When a flash of truth showed him the real advocate of one man's right to enslave another, he was dumb. The banner of popular sovereignty smote pleasantly upon the sight. When Lincoln reversed it, and men read the true inscription, they saw that it was the signal of discord, oppression, and violence. There were old stains upon that gay piece of bunting; stains of blood from the cabin hearths of Kansas, and from the marble floor of the Senate hall; and a marvelous ill-odor of cruelty hung about it, as if it were, in fact, no better than the flag of a slave-ship. Where its shadow fell across the future of a State, civilization and humanity seemed to shrink back, and a race of bondmen and their masters thinly peopled a barren land that would have "laughed in harvests" in the light of freedom.

The Douglas dogma never has been so thoroughly refuted, as by Lincoln's speeches in those debates; and Douglas himself never suffered such entire defeat, in the eyes of the country. The truth gave the victory to Lincoln; a trick bestowed the Senatorship upon Douglas.

In May, 1859, when the amendment to the Constitution of Massachusetts, extending the term of naturalization, aroused the apprehensions of many German Republicans, Dr. Theodor Canisius, a German citizen of Illinois, addressed a letter to Lincoln, asking his opinion of the amendment, and inquiring whether he favored a fusion of the Republicans with the other elements of opposition in 1860. Writing from Springfield, Lincoln replies:

"Massachusetts is a sovereign and independent State, and I have no right to advise her in her policy. Yet, if any one is desirous to draw a conclusion as to what I would do from what she has done, I may speak without impropriety. I say, then, that so far as I understand the Massachusetts provision, I am against its adoption, not only in Illinois, but in every other place in which I have the right to oppose it. As I understand the spirit of our institutions, it is designed to promote the *elevation* of men. I am, therefore, hostile to anything that tends to their debasement. It is well known that I deplore the oppressed condition of the blacks, and it would, therefore, be very inconsistent for me to look with approval upon any measure that infringes upon the inalienable rights of white men, whether or not they are born in another land or speak a different language from our own.

" In respect to a fusion, I am in favor of it whenever it can be effected on Republican principles, but upon *no other condition*. A fusion upon any other platform would be as insane as unprincipled. It would thereby lose the whole North, while the common enemy would still have the support of the entire South. The question in relation to men is different. There are good and patriotic men and able statesmen in the South whom I would willingly support if they would place themselves on Republican ground; but I shall oppose the lowering of the Republican standard even by a *hair's-breadth*."

During the gubernatorial canvass of 1859, in Ohio, Lincoln was invited to address the people of that State, and appeared before them, at Columbus and Cincinnati, in September. The impression made was one of universal favor; and it was through the interest awakened by these speeches, that the Republican Central Committee and State officers of Ohio, were led to request copies of his debates with Douglas, for publication in book-form. The Ohioans went to hear him with full allowances for the exaggerations of Illinois enthusiasm; when they had heard him, their own admiration equaled that of the Illinoians.

It was, doubtless, with still greater surprise that New England and New York listened to him. His speech at the Cooper Institute, in the commercial and intellectual metropolis, was the most brilliant success in everything that makes such an effort successful. His audience was vast in numbers, and profoundly attentive. They found him, indeed, lank and angular in form, but of fine oratorial presence; lucid and simple in his style, vigorous in argument, speaking with a full, clear voice. He addressed appeals of reason to the sense and conscience of his hearers, and skillfully hit the humor of a critical and unfamiliar people.

CHAPTER IX.

THE Republican National Convention, which assembled at Chicago on the 16th of May, was no less marked by a diversity of preferences than a unity of interests. In three days it accomplished its work—the conciliation of men and the assimilation of sections on minor points of difference. In three days Abraham Lincoln was nominated, and the armies of the irrepressible conflict were united under the banner of the man who was the first to utter that great truth, which all men felt.*

I need hardly recount the incidents of that Convention, of which the great event has proven so satisfactory. They are all fresh in the minds of the people, who watched, hour by hour, and day by day, the proceedings of one of the most distinguished bodies which ever assembled in this country.

The Convention met in Chicago without factitious advantages. The failure of the Democracy to nominate at Charleston left the Republicans in the dark as to the champion whom they were to combat, and there was nothing to be gained by the choice of a man with reference to a Democratic probability.

---

* See Lincoln's speech at Springfield, June 17, 1858.

What lay before the Convention, then, was the task of choosing a positive man embodying decided Republican principles, whose strength and decision of opinions should attract one side of the party, while nothing in his history should repel the other.

Up to the time of the third ballot, which resulted in the nomination of Abraham Lincoln, all the indications were favorable to the success of William H. Seward. That great man, whom no fortuity can lessen in the proud regard of the party, had rallied to his cause a host of friends—attached, powerful, vigilant.   These came to Chicago, and into the Convention, with a solid strength that swept everything before it.

Mr. Lincoln was the only candidate upon whom a considerable number of those who opposed Mr. Seward from policy, were united ; but it was not until after two votes of sentiment that a sufficient force was diverted from other favorites to swell Mr. Lincoln's vote into a majority.

The leader of the New York delegation, who had worked so faithfully for Mr. Seward, was the first to move the unanimous nomination of Lincoln, which was done amid demonstrations of the wildest enthusiasm, in the wigwam of the Convention and throughout the city of Chicago.   At the same instant the lightning flashed the tidings throughout the land, and in a thousand towns and cities the cannon thundered back the jubilant responses of the people.

The fact of his nomination was at once telegraphed
    8

to Lincoln, at Springfield. He received it with characteristic quiet. Seated in the *Illinois State Journal* office,
talking over the Convention with a number of friends, he
was approached by the telegraphic operator. "Mr. Lincoln, you are nominated for the Presidency." Lincoln
took the proffered dispatch in silence, and read it. At
length he folded it carefully, and saying to the exuber-
ant bystanders, "There is a little woman down street
who would like to know something about this," went
home to communicate the news to his wife.

The little city of Springfield was in a phrensy of excitement; and that night all the streets were ablaze
with bonfires, and thronged by the rejoicing Republicans. The faet of the nomination of the man whom
every one of his fellow-townsmen regarded with pride,
was excuse enough for all sorts of vocal and pyrotechnic
extravagances.

The next day, the excursion train arrived from Chicago with a large number of delegates, and the Committee appointed by the Convention to make Lincoln
officially acquainted with his nomination.

The deputation was received at Mr. Lincoln's house,
and when the guests had assembled in the parlor, Mr.
Ashmun, the President of the Convention, said :

"I have, sir, the honor, in behalf of the gentlemen
who are present, a Committee appointed by the Republican Convention, recently assembled at Chicago, to dis-
charge a most pleasant duty. We have come, sir, under

a vote of instructions to that Committee, to notify you that you have been selected by the Convention of the Republicans at Chicago, for President of the United States. They instruct us, sir, to notify you of that selection, and that Committee deem it not only respectful to yourself, but appropriate to the important matter which they have in hand, that they should come in person, and present to you the authentic evidence of the action of that Convention ; and, sir, without any phrase which shall either be considered personally plauditory to yourself, or which shall have any reference to the principles involved in the questions which are connected with your nomination, I desire to present to you the letter which has been prepared, and which informs you of the nomination, and with it the platform, resolutions, and sentiments which the Convention adopted. Sir, at your convenience we shall be glad to receive from you such a response as it may be your pleasure to give us."

To this address Mr. Lincoln listened with grave attention, and replied :

"MR. CHAIRMAN AND GENTLEMEN OF THE COMMITTEE:

" I tender to you and through you to the Republican National Convention, and all the people represented in it, my profoundest thanks for the high honor done me, which you now formally announce. Deeply, and even painfully sensible of the great responsibility which is inseparable from this high honor—a responsibility which

I could almost wish had fallen upon some one of the far more eminent men and experienced statesmen whose distinguished names were before the Convention, I shall, by your leave, consider more fully the resolutions of the Convention denominated the platform, and without unnecessary or unreasonable delay, respond to you, Mr. Chairman, in writing, not doubting that the platform will be found satisfactory, and the nomination gratefully accepted.

" And now I will not longer defer the pleasure of taking you, and each of you, by the hand."

After this response, it is proper to immediately add the letter in which Mr. Lincoln has since formally accepted the nomination :

" SPRINGFIELD, ILLINOIS, May 23, 1860.

" HON. GEORGE ASHMUN,

' President of the Republican National Convention :

" SIR : I accept the nomination tendered me by the Convention over which you presided, of which I am formally apprised in the letter of yourself and others acting as a Committee of the Convention for that purpose. The declaration of principles and sentiments which accompanies your letter meets my approval, and it shall be my care not to violate it, or disregard it in any part.

" Imploring the assistance of Divine Providence, and with due regard to the views and feelings of all who were represented in the Convention, to the rights of all

the states and territories and people of the nation, to
the inviolability of the Constitution, and the perpetual
union, harmony, and prosperity of all, I am most happy
to co-operate for the practical success of the principles
declared by the Convention.

"Your obliged friend and fellow-citizen,

"ABRAHAM LINCOLN."

People who visit Mr. Lincoln are pleased no less at
the simple and quiet style in which he lives, than at the
perfect ease and cordiality with which they are received.
The host puts off half his angularity at home, or hides
it beneath the mantle of hospitality; and the hostess
is found "a pattern of lady-like courtesy and polish,"
who "converses with freedom and grace, and is thoroughly *au fait* in all the little amenities of society," and
who will "do the honors of the White House with
appropriate grace." Intellectually, she is said to be
little her husband's inferior.

Lincoln's residence is a comfortable two-story frame
house, not now new in appearance, and situated in the
northeast part of Springfield. The grounds about it,
which are not spacious, are neatly and tastefully kept.

Mr. Lincoln's political room is an apartment in the
State House, at the door of which you knock uncere-
moniously. A sturdy voice calls out, "Come in!" and
you find yourself in the presence of a man who rises
to the hight of six feet three inches, as you enter.
He shakes you with earnest cordiality by the hand—

receiving you as in the old days he would have received a friend who called upon him at his farm-work; for those who have always known him, say that, though Lincoln is now more distinguished, he has always been a great man, and his simple and hearty manners have undergone no change. You find him, in physique, thin and wiry, and he has an appearance of standing infirmly upon his feet, which often deceived those who contended with him in the wrestle, in his younger days.

The great feature of the man's face is his brilliant and piercing eye, which has never been dimmed by any vice, great or small. His rude and vigorous early life contributed to strengthen the robust constitution which he inherited, and he is now, at fifty, in the prime of life, with rugged health, though bearing, in the lines of his face, the trace of severe and earnest thought.

The biographer's task ends here, and he does not feel that any speculations with regard to the future would be of great worth or pertinence, though conjecture is easy and a prophetic reputation possible. He prefers to leave the future of Lincoln to Providence and to the people, who often make history without the slightest respect to the arrangements of sagacious writers.

INDEX